BOOKS ★ CLOTH[ES]

The Complete Guide to Internet Shopping

RRP £9.95

★ Huge listing of the Web's best shops ★
★ How to buy on the Net ★
★ Avoiding frauds and scams ★

Published by Paragon Publishing Ltd
Paragon House, St Peter's Road,
Bournemouth, UK BH1 2JS
Tel: 01202 299900
Fax: 01202 299955
http://www.paragon.co.uk

All rights reserved. No part of this publication may be reproduced, stored in a retrieval system, or transmitted in any form whatsoever without the written consent of the publishers. This book may not be lent, re-sold hired out or otherwise disposed of by way of trade in any form of binding or cover other than that in which it is published.

While every effort has been made to ensure that the information contained in **The Complete Guide to Internet Shopping** is accurate, Paragon Publishing Ltd makes no warranty, either expressed or implied, as to its quality, performance, merchantability or fitness for any purpose.

Managing Editor: Geoff Harris
Contributors: Sandra Vogel,
Shaun Marin, Paul Russell, Jo Chipchase
Designer: Paul Ridley
Production: Jo Cole
Printed by: Caledonian International Book Manufacturing Ltd, Westerhill Road, Bishopbriggs, Glasgow, G64 2QR
Published by: Paragon Publishing Ltd

CONTENTS

Chapter 1
The Benefits of Online Shopping 9

Chapter 2
General Tips 15

Chapter 3
Bargain Shopping 21

Chapter 4
Shopping With £10 35

Chapter 5
Small Businesses 47

Chapter 6
Passion for Fashion 59

Chapter 7
A-Z Shopping Sites 73

Appendix
Useful Resources 251

The complete guide to **Internet shopping**

GET ONLINE CHEAPER, FASTER AND EASIER

Practical Internet is the magazine that skips the hype and gets straight down to explaining, in plain English, how to get the best out of the Net without drowning in the trash. Every month, *Practical Internet* is crammed with features, reviews and advice on everything of interest to the dial-up user. So whether you want to squeeze more speed from your modem, cut your phone costs, get to grips with email, the Web and newsgroups, or avoid paying for calls to your technical support line, *Practical Internet* is all you need.

For more information turn to page 122 in the magazine or call 01202 200200

Published by Paragon Publishing Ltd
Paragon House, St Peter's Road,
Bournemouth, UK, BH1 2JS
Tel: 01202 299900
Fax: 01202 299955
http://www.paragon.co.uk

INTRODUCTION

Shopping online comes as a bit of a culture shock to most of us. It seems strange, alien, perhaps even a little too futuristic to make purchases using a computer. But it really shouldn't feel this way, especially when the separate elements involved are similar, if not identical, to things we do each and every day.

Today, we all use cash machines to deal with our finances, and think nothing about letting these computers balance our accounts and tell us whether or not we can have any money. But imagine telling people 50, 40 or even 20 years ago that they wouldn't go into a bank to withdraw funds – that they'd use a hole in the wall instead.

Admittedly, it's a bit unusual choosing certain goods, such as clothes, just by looking at them on a computer screen. But if you think about it, we regularly order things without ever seeing them first hand. Catalogues have been doing great business for years, without ever feeling the need to come round our house with a big lorry full of stuff to let us try everything on first.

In this book we hope to show you how easy it is to shop online, and we'll address any fears you have about security. We'll show you the best places to find some bargains, and if you want to start small, what you can expect to buy by just spending a tenner. We'll also show you how the Net is being used by small businesses to encourage custom, and how the fashion moguls are creating their very own online fashion emporiums. After all this, you'll find an A-Z directory of great shopping sites where you will have plenty of opportunity to exercise those credit cards and spend some money. So read on and get shopping!

CHAPTER ONE: THE BENEFITS OF SHOPPING ONLINE

THE BENEFITS OF SHOPPING ONLINE

There are a host of benefits to shopping online which should convince even the most hardened sceptic to give it a whirl

CHAPTER ONE: THE BENEFITS OF SHOPPING ONLINE

Are you intrigued by online shopping? Feel like dipping your toe in the virtual shopping malls? Well you should, as the pros far outweigh the cons. It's convenient, easy and you will probably make some savings along the way. People are still quite unsure about how secure the whole process is, but we'll explain all that's involved. Despite the concerns that some people have about ordering goods over the Net, more and more people are taking to the online malls, and here are some of the reasons why:

- **Cost**

It may be filthy, but lucre is what makes the world go round, and if you can save some, so much the better. You're not going to make phenomenal savings by shopping online, but you can expect to save at least something. Buying goods straight from a manufacturer means you are cutting out the middleman, so there is extra money floating around. If you buy from abroad, a strong pound will work in your favour. Everyone's a winner!

The only thing we would point out about buying online, is be aware of shipping costs. You could be making a real saving on the actual product, but if you have to pay a small fortune to receive your purchase, it might be cheaper to buy it from your local shop.

- **Convenience**

There's no denying it – the Net is an excellent and convenient way to shop. Instead of traipsing for miles around the shops, you just have to shuffle along to the computer and sit down. You can shoot from Slough to Seattle to Sidcup with just a click of a mouse.

If shopping means juggling kids with dogs and prams, going online will save you the trouble of rounding up the troops for a swift walk around the shops. And if you're not particularly mobile, there are no awkward steps and doors to negotiate.

One of the main benefits of shopping online is that you can do it whenever you like. Whether it's the middle of the day or the middle of the night, you can get online and purchase yourself some goodies.

- **Range**

There's a vast range of products online, and you'll be amazed at what you can find. Instead of running all over town looking for that perfect present, all you have to do is pop along to the relevant site for what you want to buy, and then click a few

CHAPTER ONE: THE BENEFITS OF SHOPPING ONLINE

buttons. Also, if you have a penchant for the obscure, you're bound to find loads of odd goodies that you wouldn't be able to find in your local shops.

- **Security**

So given all these advantages, why aren't high street retailers reeling from the assaults of online rivals? Basically because millions of potential customers don't buy over the Net because they're worried about the safety of online transactions, especially via credit card. This is a shame, because as long as you buy from a reputable site (such as the ones listed in this book), online shopping is as safe as any other kind. It's ironic that the people who never buy CDs via the Web because they're worried about their credit card being charged by 'hackers' will happily hand the card over to a dodgy looking waiter in a restaurant, or read out the card number over a mobile phone.

Encryption technology

The key reason that the Web is a safe rather than an unsafe place to do business is encryption. Encryption systems have been specially designed to make sure that sensitive information like credit card numbers are encoded when they are transmitted over the Internet, and then decoded when they reach their destination. The actual encryption is different for each purchase, and only you and the vendor have the key to unlock the code for your particular transaction.

Encryption systems basically scramble, or encode, sensitive information such as credit card numbers sent over the Net. The information is then decoded when it reaches its destination, and each encryption is different for each purchase. What's more, only you and the vendor have the key to unlock the encryption. Sounds complicated, but relax – you don't encode the card details yourself, it's all done for you if you have a relatively modern Web browser and buy from a 'secure server.' A secure server is basically a big computer at the vendor's end which allows you to transmit confidential information over the Net. Once you connect to a secure server, a secure channel is set up, and all data passing through that channel is encrypted. Many secure servers use a technology called Secure Socket Layer (SSL). You and the vendor must have a security certificate, which your software (a Web browser, for instance) sends the vendor and the vendor's software sends back to you. You and the vendor can then encrypt/decrypt data as required, via this certificate. The best online stores proudly display that they support SSL, or other encryption systems.

In practise, this system means that it is impossible for someone to intervene between you and the vendor you are visiting, steal your credit card details, and use your number to make their own purchases. This is because your credit card number, and other personal details, will be in a code that they can't break.

The caveat to this, of course, is that you should only divulge your credit card details to a vendor who states categorically that they use encryption. In the early days of online shopping, many vendors simply used forms-enabled email systems to transmit your credit card details across the vast space of the Internet. In security terms, this is a bit like giving your credit card details over the phone. You've no idea who might be tapping in and grabbing your details in order to use them illicitly. The chances of such a situation occurring are pretty slim, but they are there.

Today, all serious vendors should use encryption, and they should make this clear at their Web sites. The best rule of thumb is that if you can't determine easily that encryption is used, steer clear of divulging your details. The best Web sites will proudly display information about encryption, alongside stuff about returns and cancellation policies.

Ready, SET, go?

A new secure payment system called Secure Electronic Transactions (SET) could replace SSL as a popular way of ensuring the security of online transactions. SET was put forward by Mastercard and Visa, and is backed by IBM and Microsoft. It works like this – your credit card company gives you an SET 'wallet,' basically a certificate that proves your identity. You install this software certificate on your computer. When you want to buy something over the Net, you send a message to the vendor's bank which tells it who you are. Meanwhile the vendor sends a message requesting payment. The bank checks the details and confirms the transaction with the merchant. One advantage is that the bank never knows what you have bought (although it knows how much you are paying) and the vendor is never privy to your credit card details. SET is still at the testing stage, but

CHAPTER ONE: THE BENEFITS OF SHOPPING ONLINE

pundits predict that most online transactions will be based on it in a few years.

CHAPTER TWO: GENERAL TIPS

GENERAL TIPS

Although people are gradually getting more used to the idea of buying goods online, it is still a good idea to take a couple of precautions. We've compiled a list of essential tips to help you on your way

CHAPTER TWO: GENERAL TIPS

Essential tips

If you're still a bit worried about buying online, here are a few tips that will ensure your shopping trip on the Net is a safe one.

• Use a secure browser
Make sure that your browser complies with industry standards. Look out for Secure Sockets Layer (SSL) or Secure Electronic Transaction (SET). These standards make sure that your purchase information you send over the Net is scrambled and encrypted, so only the people who should see the information actually get to see it. The latest versions of Internet Explorer and Netscape Navigator are fine.

• Choose your companies carefully
If you visit a Web site and it all appears a bit sketchy, don't order anything. You wouldn't hand your money over to some dodgy geezer you met on the street, and you shouldn't order hundreds of pounds worth of stuff from a Web site that looks like it has been thrown together in five minutes. If there are no contact details, be on your guard. See if they can send you a catalogue so you know that the company isn't going to disappear overnight. Also make sure that you check out the returns and refunds policies so you know where you stand if things aren't to your liking.

• Keep a record
Always keep a copy of your purchase order and confirmation number for your order. Some sites, such as CDnow (**http://www.cdnow.com**) will have special facilities so you can track what stage your order is at online. This is obviously a good thing, as you can put your mind at rest that your goods are actually getting to you. Also, merchants sometimes send you emails with information about what's going on with your order. You should also pay particular attention to your bank and credit card statements, so that if any discrepancies do occur, you spot them and get them sorted out quickly.

• Methods of payment
Be aware that you don't necessarily have to pay for goods on your credit card. Although most of the talk about online shopping concentrates on credit card payments, there are other methods that can be used, too. If you are shopping from a site based in

CHAPTER TWO: GENERAL TIPS

the UK, your choices should really be greater than simply the credit card option. Some of these other methods are entirely offline, giving you the advantage of using the Web to find the goods you want, and then using a payment method that suits you best. Look for the following:

Fax
Some Web sites include an order form, which you can complete within your browser, print out, and fax. With a fax modem or traditional fax machine, this lets you deliver a formatted order immediately, using credit card details, but avoids the need to send the details directly over the Internet.

Phone
Any Web site selling goods that doesn't offer phone ordering to people in its own country is doing itself a great disservice. Look for the phone number option if you want to stick to a method of payment that you are well experienced in using.

Invoice
Some Web sites will take an order and bill you for the goods. The chances are that they might not despatch until they receive payment, so turnaround time will be a little bit longer, but a bill means you can write a cheque in payment, and that you have a record of the sale.

eCHARGE: a new approach to buying online

A new system currently being tested in the US should be on its way over here soon, and it could be just what you are looking for if you still have concerns about using your credit card.

Called eCHARGE, the system lets users buy goods online and charge the cost to their phone bills. In effect, it turns your phone bill into a sort of credit card.

Technically, the eCHARGE system is as easy to use as sending a credit card payment down the line – almost. All it requires in addition to the single 'click to buy' arrangement, is a new connection to a separate service, which actually records the cost of the goods you want to buy onto your phone bill. The connection, and reconnection to your ISP if you want it, is automatic.

CHAPTER TWO: GENERAL TIPS

eCHARGE is secure because no personal details at all are sent to the vendor. The downside, though, is that it costs. Users have to pay a transaction fee that is linked to the value of the goods purchased. Still, if a few pence on the cost of your goods is what it takes to deliver confidence, some people will undoubtedly be taken with the idea.

CHAPTER TWO: GENERAL TIPS

CHAPTER THREE: BARGAIN SHOPPING

BARGAIN SHOPPING

If you're after a bargain, the Net is a great place to come. Sandra Vogel looks at the sites where you could make a saving

CHAPTER THREE: BARGAIN SHOPPING

An ever-increasing number of people are using the Internet to buy goods and services. Special gifts and presents, and day-to-day items are readily available to purchase over the Net, and once people realise how easy it is to shop online, they are often hooked. As a bonus, using the Internet to buy things is sometimes cheaper than using traditional retail outlets. Often, Net shoppers find themselves quids in over their high street counterparts, and with a whole world's worth of shops to choose from, the range of goods and services is greater, too.

It is little wonder, then, that surveys often show that shopping online is one of the major growth areas of the Internet – one that will, quite probably, help to shape the future of retail trade in years to come. It makes sense. On the one hand you have punters who can save time, effort and money using the Net to shop, while on the other you have a technology that is constantly reducing the costs of setting up an online store. It is possible for a savvy Internet operator to get a shop going for around £500 these days.

Creatures of habit

But even though many of us know that Internet shopping can be cheaper, faster and more effective than any other kind, it is not really booming at the moment – why? The one thing that is really holding shopping on the Internet back is public perception of the security issues involved in using the medium. Encryption is obviously very important in persuading people to shop online, but there is another factor that stops people from using the Internet for shopping – habit. There are parallels in other areas of shopping life. How many of you know that the supermarkets are always full at 10am on a Saturday? Most of you. Yet how many of you still insist on doing your own weekly shop at that time? Tuesday evening is the ideal time to avoid the crowds. You know that as well as we do, but you are also probably as bad as us at taking advantage of it.

It's the same with online shopping. We know that we can get the new CD we want online more easily than making a special trip to the shop, or that we can get the wine that goes particularly well with the special meal we're preparing from the Web in about 10 minutes instead of traipsing round the shops looking for it. When put like that, you know Internet shopping makes sense, it's just a matter of breaking that habit.

CHAPTER THREE: BARGAIN SHOPPING

Over the next few pages we show you how easy it is to go shopping online, and why you should think about doing it. There are some Web sites listed to get you started, and which might even save you a bit of money. Shop on!

THE ONLINE SHOPPING EXPERIENCE

Where to shop on the Internet to find the best bargains, most useful services and original gifts

Victoria Wine
http://www.victoriawine.co.uk

This is a centralised version of the high street store, but with a difference. By visiting this online shop, you can save yourself the hassle of trying to find the items you want by searching specific branches. There are no real price savings to be had here over shop costs, but the convenience rating is high, and the site makes a point of dropping in special offers that you might just miss if you are not a regular visitor to the high street stores.

Tesco Online
http://www.tesco.co.uk

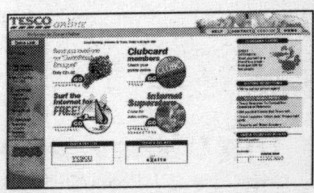

Online supermarket shopping is a bit of a let-down at the moment. Even though Tesco is the leader among the national chains, the Internet Superstore is only available if you live in one of a small number of selected postcodes. The software simply throws you out if you don't live in one of the districts served. But there is a large online gift shop that will allow you to select

CHAPTER THREE: BARGAIN SHOPPING

items and have them delivered to other people. The range runs from choccies to toys, books to balloon flights. Not stunning, but a move in the right direction.

Q Shop
http://www.qonline.co.uk

This is an online shopping site, courtesy of Q magazine. It offers chart CDs, videos, gig tickets, merchandise, games and books of the kind that Q readers will enjoy.
There is plenty here to browse through, and the interface is well designed and neat. The prices aren't bad, either. Where music is concerned, the back-catalogue is extensive, so building up a collection of a particular artist or band could be made very easy here. As a bonus you can link straight in and check out the magazine when you've finished shopping.

August Florist
http://www.augustflorist.com

The August Florist virtual shop delivers flowers worldwide via Interflora. Flowers are never cheap, and two red roses in a box will set you back £15, but hey, if you order before noon your delivery is made within the UK the same day. Add a fiver to the price if you want the flowers to go abroad. You can order online, or use the prominently displayed phone number if you prefer.

The Disney Store
http://disney.go.com/Shopping/

If you can't possibly do without the cutesy stuff from the latest Disney movie – which might not yet be released in the UK – there is no need

CHAPTER THREE: BARGAIN SHOPPING

to traipse to the country's largest shopping centres for a Disney store. You can just go to the online version and buy direct. You'll find that the gifts are organised by category, character, movie, and age group, so finding what you want is easy. And, of course, the range is greater here than in your average British Disney store.

Gift Store UK
http://www.giftstore.co.uk

This UK-based site is intended as a one-stop shop for buying something for a friend or relative. If you are short of ideas for what to buy that loved one, this is a good place to visit, as it offers both standard and not so standard gifts. There are the usual things like flowers and choccies (please send either to us immediately), as well as games, toys, computer games, music, video, and even, rather oddly, juggling balls. Online ordering is easy, you can choose cards to send with your presents to the UK and abroad, and there is even a gift wrapping service.

Etoys
http://www.etoy.com/html/et_home.shtml

Another American Web site, this toy store beats the UK's Hamleys and Toys R Us shops hands down, simply because it gets the toys delighting American kiddies long before they appear this side of the Atlantic. Toys are organised by age group, brand and subject. Order direct to ensure that those things that are out of stock, or simply unavailable locally, get to your little darlings in time for their birthdays or even Christmas.

CHAPTER THREE: BARGAIN SHOPPING

FragranceNet
http://www.fragrancenet.com/zhtml

This is a very large Web site considering that it is entirely devoted to perfume. There are special offers that change regularly, as well as constantly featured colognes for men and women, including all the top brands.

Much of the smelly stuff on offer is available at large discounts. Given that you are charged in dollars and the pound is doing well at the moment you could be in for a double winner if you choose this site for your shopping. Use the on-board international currency converter if you need to check on just how much money you can save.

As a special service the site will automatically remind you of any important birthdays and anniversaries, so you will never forget to send that perfumed pressie again.

Beyond.com
http://www.beyond.com/internet.htm

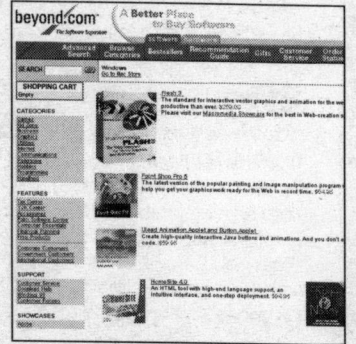

Offering 21,000 software titles, this site could well have the application you've been searching for all over town.

You can look for particular titles or browse categories – Games, Utilities, Business software – it is all here.

As an added incentive if you are desperate, some software is available for immediate download. Prices are in dollars, but they are usually cheaper than the US RRP, and so chances are they will beat the UK one, too.

CHAPTER THREE: BARGAIN SHOPPING

The Amazing Interactive T-Shirt Company

http://www.jerseyvirtual.net/shirts/

This really is an odd shopping site and no mistake. It's an online replication of those shops that put your face – or your cat or dog or anything you have a photo of – onto a T shirt. In this case, the idea is that you give the manufacturers a URL of a Web page, perhaps your own or one with some particularly cool graphics, and they put it onto a T-shirt or sweatshirt for you. As a bonus, they'll let you know if they think the page is unsuitable for a T-shirt. The service isn't cheap, but it is probably unique.

Worldwide Exotic Seed Company

http://www.seedman.com/WWseeds.html

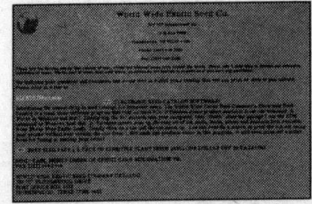

If you're a gardener and you are into exotic species of plants, this is the place to come for the seeds. You can view the catalogue online, or download it to browse at your leisure, and then partake in secure online ordering when you've made your choices. The Web site doesn't look all that good, and it probably won't appeal to everyone, but the product range is plentiful.

Interactive Music and Video Shop

http://www.imvs.com/

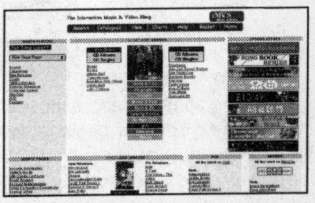

This impressive American-based site hosts one of the

CHAPTER THREE: BARGAIN SHOPPING

most extensive collections of music and video for sale on the Net. Whatever you want, you will most likely be able to find it within the 180,000 items here – including hard to get DVD titles.

Although based in the US, as soon as you try to buy anything, you will be taken to a UK site, with prices in sterling to make it easier to spot and buy any bargains.

Innovations
http://www.innovations.co.uk

Innovations, you know, those catalogues that drop out of Sunday newspaper supplements as you're walking back from the newsagent? They're full of techy gadgets and things to make your life easier, such as special knives for cutting grapefruits, pillows to rest your weary head while on a aeroplane, and fancy barometers that forecast rain. Well, now you don't have to wait for the paper version to fall out of a newspaper – pop online and buy direct.

The Kite Shop
http://www.kiteshop.co.uk

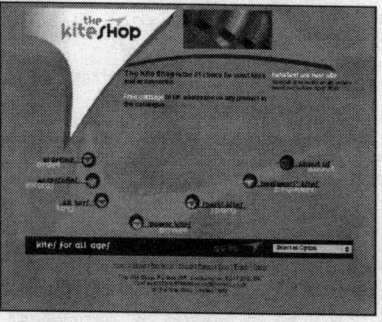

If you are into kites you'll know that they are not just a hobby – more a way of life. The Kite Shop has just about every variety you can imagine available, covering all prices and a vast variety of styles and uses. A special section on kites for beginners will get you going, but there are also kite buggies (to pull you along the beach), sports kites, power kites, you name it.

Entertainment Express

http://www.entexpress.com

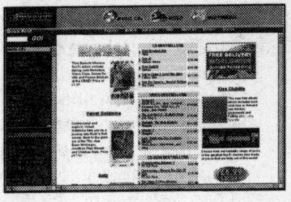

Entertainment Express is a Web site from the Kingfisher Group (Woolies, MVC, Superdrug etc.) selling CDs, videos, and computer games. The site has a fairly impressive range of titles on offer, but, just as in any high street shop, the emphasis is on the big chart successes of the moment, and there are plenty of promotions and price cuts associated with the latest titles.

One of the major features that makes Entertainment Express stand out from its competition is that it offers next day delivery, with free package and posting – meaning it is only a day slower than popping down the shops to buy your music and videos.

Secure shopping success

If you are going to send your credit card details over the Internet, make sure that a secure system is being used. The Web site should make this very clear in its information to customers.

Check the full cost of your goods. Don't be lured by incredibly cheap prices on the first page without first finding out what the postage costs are. Remember, that just as printed catalogues can do the dirty when it comes to charging heavily for postage, so can online services. Even if postage doesn't cost a packet, it can still erode any cash savings you might make online.

Check on the cancellation policy. Some online shopping sites let you cancel orders up to a certain period after placing the order. Check to find out what the rules are before rushing in – but the bottom line is don't order if you aren't sure you want to buy.

Consider insurance. If you are buying breakable items can you take out insurance? Don't rely on your standard credit card provider to give insurance for online purchases. The law is sketchy in this area, and has not been tested enough in court for there to be any certainty about how it applies. If you can't

CHAPTER THREE: BARGAIN SHOPPING

get insurance and are worried, try to find out what the packaging is actually like to learn how much protection it will give. A quality sales team will respond to email requests for information like this. Keep copies of the information you are given – just in case you need to make a complaint later.

If you are buying food, check on the delivery turnaround times. You want to make sure that your eatables arrive safely, are fresh and not past their use-by date.

Look for quality customer information. Just as there are many rip-off merchants in the real world of consumer goods, there are some to be found on the Web. In the end you'll have to use your own judgement to work out if a seller is worth using, but if they have high standards of customer information at the site you should be in a reasonably good position.

Cost vs convenience

Your head might tell you that buying on the Internet should save you cash, but don't get too excited. Shopping online isn't always cheaper than shopping in the high street, and even where there are cost savings they are likely to be of a few pence rather than pounds. For example, the Madonna CD, Ray of Light, costs £13.99 in HMV and a cheaper £12.82 at the new Q store, but there are shipping costs to be added that bring it closer to the shop price.

Buying abroad might be a good bet at the moment, particularly if the pound is strong against a foreign currency as you could make a considerable saving in the conversion. But that old chestnut of 'what the market will bear,' helps keep online prices relatively healthy. Generally speaking, prices in any market are set at a level that people will pay. Sometimes online shops charge close to shop prices simply because buying via the Web is a lot easier than using conventional retail outlets and they figure you'll pay for the convenience. In the end, maybe you will. When doing your own research into prices before buying goods online, if you find they are more expensive, then the convenience factor could come into play.

As a general rule, though, if you are looking for bargains, the more you buy at any one online store, the more you save, as shipping costs are generally reduced on larger quantities of goods.

CHAPTER THREE: BARGAIN SHOPPING

THE MALLS, THE MALLS!

Online shopping malls are a great place to start your online shopping journey. You can go along and browse all the shops that are housed in one site. Here are some of the best.

Barclay Square
http://www.barclaysquare.co.uk

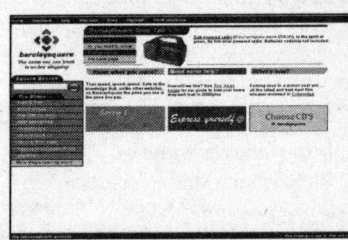

One of the UK's first virtual shopping malls, this is still a good place for beginners to come, despite having been around for a while. The idea behind a virtual mall is to bring shops together in one place. Most of those here are large and well known, you can stop off at big names like Argos, Toys R Us, and Victoria Wine for example. But what else is good about Barclay Square is that if you are new to online shopping there is plenty of useful information here, especially on subjects such as security issues.

Buy It Online
http://www.buyitonline.com

This mall is American rather than British, and it is quite simply vast. Where you might find a few hundred shops in our biggest real malls, this one offers no less than 30,000 online stores.

Of course, most are American, but buying things from the States can sometimes prove cheaper than sourcing them from the UK, and, of course, a lot of goods simply aren't available over here. You can search the sites by category or keywords, and there are often ideas for special events.

CHAPTER THREE: BARGAIN SHOPPING

UK Shopping City
http://www.ukshops.co.uk

OK, so this isn't the best looking Internet site in the world, but we shouldn't judge it on that criteria alone. The majority of the sites are actually hosted by UK Shopping City – there's still room to rent, by the way – and there's plenty of choice. There seems to be a pleasant mix between household names and small online-only traders. Companies represented include Comet, Argos, Motor Net Direct and the disappointing Marks & Spencer site.

Virgin Shopping Channel
http://www.virgin.net

Although not strictly a shopping mall, Virgin's Shopping Channel offers you a wide range of 'recommended' online stores and offers you complete protection if your credit card details are ripped off while shopping there. As Virgin Net Chief Executive David Clarke told us when we interviewed him in Practical Internet issue 17: "The risk to us is quite minimal, because actually the number of individual credit card frauds is pretty low."

Stores currently trading through Virgin include Amazon.com, iMVS and Unbeatable, for online electronic goods.

CHAPTER THREE: BARGAIN SHOPPING

CHAPTER FOUR: SHOP WITH £10

SHOP WITH £10

There's bargains on that there Internet! We stuck a tenner on Shaun Marin's credit card and sent him on an online shopping spree. This is what he found...

CHAPTER FOUR: SHOP WITH £10

Buying over the Net via a secure server is a lot less risky than reading out your credit card details to a faceless voice at the end of a phone line. Generally, your details stay on the seller's server for no more than a few seconds, before the information is sent off to a bank to deal with. No human eye ever sees the information, let alone gets a chance to note it down and use it.

Also, more high street shops are now trading on the Net. Dixons, Argos, Tesco, and Virgin, to name a few. Come on, how much more trustworthy can you get? You probably give these people your credit card details on fairly regular basis anyway.

What we need to do is get our collective feet wet. Just dip a toe into the world of e-commerce. A quick fix to get the feel of it, and who knows – you may like it. So let's start with a small amount. Nothing too big or too risky. Perhaps £10. Ready? Then let's shop.

MUSIC, BOOKS AND VIDEO
Entertainment from the Net stores

An area where the Internet has its virtual foot firmly wedged in our collective front door is in selling books, music and videos. It's debatable whether the plethora of Web sites devoted to these products came before or after the public demand for them, but the competition certainly makes for some bargain buys.

For starters, we're heading off to Waterstone's – **http://www.waterstones.co.uk** – the online home of one of Britain's largest chain of booksellers. This impressive site has around a million titles on its database, and we managed to locate a copy of Ian M Banks' Consider Phlebas for £5.59. With postal charges – £1.50 for UK orders – this comes to just under £7, which is not bad at all if you live somewhere without a local branch. It'll take about a week to get to you.

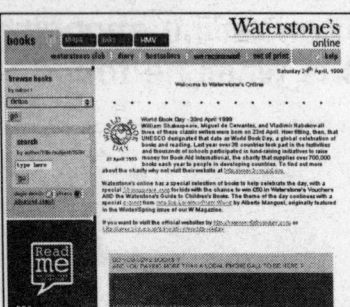

For more obscure titles or American

CHAPTER FOUR: SHOP WITH £10

editions there's Amazon.com – **http://www.amazon.com**. You'll find loads of lovely literature just waiting to be discovered.

Nearer home, we snapped up a copy of Graham Greene's memoirs, Sort of Life, for the discount price of £6.29 plus £1.50 postage from the Internet Bookshop – **http://www.bookshop.co.uk**. Again, quite good for a book not readily available in most high street shops, and it arrives within a couple of days. Both Waterstone's and the Internet Bookshop offer free postage after you go above a certain limit – in both cases this is around the £40 mark, which is above of our £10 limit.

Pick and mix

But man can not live by the written word alone. Bring on the music! Apart from the bargains and convenience, one of our favourite things about shopping on the Internet is being able to buy CDs that you just can't get hold of in this country by any other means. We've been after a copy of More Specials, the fantastic second album for the eighties Coventry Ska outfit, but we didn't want to pay £20 for it on import in our local shop. We tried a couple of UK sites first off, but no joy. Thankfully the impressive CDnow – **http://www.cdnow.com** – not only had it in stock, but actually in a sale for $10.49. With the $6.96 postage, this comes in a few pence over out £10 limit, but we're dead pleased we've found it.

Another great feature about buying music on the Net is that

CHAPTER FOUR: SHOP WITH £10

the sites tend to have a wealth of background information and links connected with the album in which you're interested. Some sites post reviews from people who have bought the item, which is particularly useful if you're interested in something you haven't heard before. Often you can listen to downloadable snippets, as well.

Talking of which, Music Boulevard has taken an even more revolutionary approach to selling music. From its site – **http://www.musicblvd.com** – you can choose between buying a CD or downloading an MP3 file, which you can then write onto your own CD, or upload into one of the new MPEG players. There are only 60 tracks on sale here at the moment, but expect this side of the business to grow. At $0.99, each these tracks are a bargain, and, of course, there's no postage to worry about either.

Another unusual way of buying music is offered by CDuctive – **http://www.cductive.com**. This company allows you to make your own custom CD, which is then posted to you. At $4.99 for the first track and $0.99 for each subsequent one we worked out – taking into account the $4.99 postage – that we could have seven tracks. And if we went for the longest ones we would end up with an almost-full CD of very diverse music.

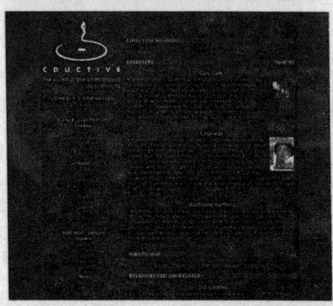

CHAPTER FOUR: SHOP WITH £10

Video surveillance

When it comes to videos and DVDs you have to be a little bit more careful where and what you buy, if only because of the separate encoding systems that are used throughout the world. Just make sure any tapes you buy are PAL VHS, and any DVDs are for the European market, unless of course you have an all-format player.

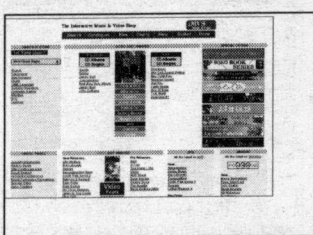

For this reason we concentrated on UK sites. Our first stop was the excellent Black Star – **http://www.blackstar. co.uk** – and we were immediately rewarded with its special offer of

the Titanic video for a mere £9.99. Quite a bargain when you consider how long the film is and that Black Star is offering free package and postage to UK addresses at the moment.

DRESSING UP

Clothes and beauty products on the Web

A more problematic area of Net shopping is buying clothes. It's vital that you look out for the site's return and refunds policy, just in case your new outfit doesn't fit or makes you look like Oliver Reed after a night on the tiles. But as long as you stick to buying items like T-shirts and hats, rather than three-piece suits and wedding dresses you should be OK.

Obviously, £10 is a bit limiting when it comes to buying clothes, so several of our favourites such as London Wide – **http://www.londonwide.co.uk** – Designers Direct – **http://www.designersdirect.com** – Red or Dead – **http://www.redordead.com** – and Diesel –

CHAPTER FOUR: SHOP WITH £10

http://www.diesel.co.uk – are ruled out immediately. For more information about these sites, see our fashion chapter starting on page 59. But there must be something out there to suit our rather limited budget.

Our first port of call in our online quest for a spot of cheap sartorial elegance was NetSale – http://www.netsale.co.uk. Unfortunately, even among the bargains here there was nothing in our price range. At least not in mens or ladies wear. But there was quite a lot here for kids. You can pick up a three-pack of Winnie the Pooh bodysuits for £6.99 plus £2.95 postage. Representing a saving of almost 25 per cent on RRP, and just squeezing in at under £10.

Silk and soap

At the impressive Bras Direct – **http://www.brasdirect.co.uk** – we couldn't afford any bras, but we could pick up three pairs of stockings for £2 each – as a gift, you understand. With £2.50 postage on top we could even get them sent directly to the recipient. We bookmarked the site with the intention of coming back once our credit card bill was cleared. You can make someone in your life very happy here, and there's even a men's section.

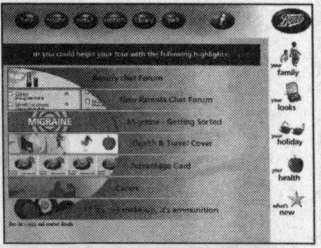

Cosmetics and beauty products are becoming more readily available as some of the major names in this area of retail move online. You can already buy goods direct from Boots – **http://www.boots.co.uk** – but the launch of Avon's UK site – **http://www.uk.avon.com** – provides shoppers with the

CHAPTER FOUR: SHOP WITH £10

opportunity to buy the company's wide range of products online – and it's quite reasonable, too. We managed to locate some shower gel and some relaxing flower-infused bubble bath, and even with delivery it came to well under a tenner.

GIFT SHOPPING
Flowers and fridge magnets...

While we're in a floral mood, we thought we'd try to send some flowers. We need to send a gift to somebody anyway, so why not from the Net. A couple of sites immediately came to mind. Our first stop was Interflora – **http://www.interflora.co.uk** – which offers a wide selection of flowers and gifts, just as you'd

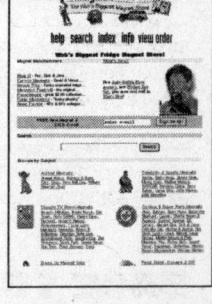

suspect. Unfortunately, the cheapest arrangements were just above our £10 ceiling, and that's without delivery. Next, we tried Flowers by Design – **http://www.flowersbydesign.co.uk** – which we featured in *Practical Internet* issue 20. Even though the arrangements here were fantastic, they were still out of our price range. Back to the drawing board on the gifts front, then. Perhaps something less traditional would be more in our price bracket.

It claims to be the 'weirdest store in cyberspace,' and to be frank the Stupid Gift shop is pretty damn odd – **http://www.stupid.com/giftshop/maingift.htm**. Among the gifts on offer was the world's ugliest puppet and some glow in the dark alien babies. In the end we decided on the Jelly brain mould. Ideal for any dinner party we thought,

CHAPTER FOUR: SHOP WITH £10

and at only $7.99, quite a bargain. But we were foiled again. Stupidly, the Stupid Gift Shop doesn't deliver outside the States yet.

Thank you, Fridge Door – **http://www.fridgedoor.com** – the world's biggest fridge magnet shop, for saving our bacon. For the miserly sum of $13, including international postage, we could pick up a nice pair of matching Kermit and Miss Piggy fridge magnets that would look great in any home. We could have chosen from a vast array of options, including South Park, Batman, Happy Days and just about any cultural icon of the 20th Century, but you can't beat the Muppets.

BACK TO BASICS
Avoid supermarket queues

When we're not shopping for gifts and luxuries, we spend much more of our money buying the basics. Monthly shops, weekly shops, daily shops. However often you take a trip to the supermarket, you have to admit, it's a pretty hellish experience. Trawling round, looking for bargains, balancing all of the major food groups, keeping your chips frozen until you can get them in the freezer, and resisting the temptation of the wines and spirits

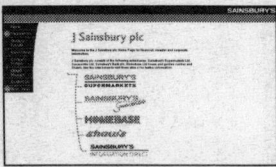

aisle – which is always at the far corner of the shop because by the time you reach it you are so in need of a drink you can't help but double the cost of your shopping by throwing as much as you can in your wobbly wheeled trolley. Even being open all night doesn't help much. Who wants to go shopping at 4am? The shop may be empty, but that's because any sane person is tucked up in bed. Now, thanks to the Internet you need never set foot in a

CHAPTER FOUR: SHOP WITH £10

supermarket again. At least not if you live in South East England or Leeds, because that's where the 11 Tesco stores currently operating online shopping are based – **http://www.tesco.co.uk/superstore**.

The service, if it's available to you, is fantastic. Anything you can buy from the shop, you can get online as well. That includes fresh meat, fish, vegetables, tins of beans, drinks and corn flakes. You won't even have to go and pick it up, as Tesco will deliver it to your door.

Not wanting to be left out Sainsbury's is also running an Internet service, although it has taken a slightly different approach to online shopping. You have to go in to one of the 9 stores that are operating the system and register there. After that you can get your products delivered to your door, again allowing you to stay in doors on wet winter weekends rather than traipsing round a supermarket.

Closing time

There are thousands of online shops on the Net at present, and more are opening on a daily basis. Although, on the whole, we've only covered the ones here that offer goods for around a tenner, you can actually buy almost anything online. There are sites dedicated to selling holidays, insurance, computers, wine, posters, fine art, electrical goods, even houses.

Once you've started buying goods this way, who knows where it will end. Even if some items aren't cheaper than you can buy in the high street – and many are – the convenience factor makes online purchasing more attractive. Online shopping is fast becoming more than just a novelty, it's turning into an ever-more viable alternative to high street shops. Why not give it a go?

PAPER SHOP

You'll be pleased to know that you can even buy your favourite Internet magazine online. The obvious place to get hold of *Practical Internet* online if you live in the UK is from the Paragon Web site – **http://www.**

CHAPTER FOUR: SHOP WITH £10

paragon.co.uk/pi. Here you can subscribe for a full year or buy back issues from £3.95 each.
But if you're off spending time in another country, try buying current issues from British Magazines Direct – **http://www.britishmagazines.com**. You can buy the latest issues and they only cost the normal cover price plus package and postage to wherever you are in the world.

GOING, GOING, GONE

As every serious shopper knows, one of the best way to pick up a real bargain is at an auction. If you're lucky you can get some top notch goods for next to nothing, just as long as you're only bidding against a few people, and you're willing to pay the reserve price.

Online auctions have been around on the other side of the Atlantic for some time now, but it can sometimes get a bit confusing bidding in a foreign currency, and many of the American Internet auctions are only open to people who live there anyway. But thanks to Quixell you can now join in, and make your bids in proper money.

The majority of the items on offer are electrical goods – such as cameras and computers – and they only stay on the market for a day at the most. This allows you to find out whether your bid has been successful, and make any counter bids necessary, without you having to log on for vast lengths of time. Signing up and bidding on Quixell is dead simple. Simply chose the product you are interested in, and then type in your bid. If you make the best bid and no one challenges you, the booty is yours.

CHAPTER FOUR: SHOP WITH £10

HOME ALONE

As well as buying tangible products over the Net, you can also purchase online services, such as access to member's only Web sites. Some of these sites are pornographic in nature, but if that's what you're into, well we're here to help. We feel we should point out, though, that no matter how safe the Internet is for transferring credit card details,
you should be wary about giving out information to some of the more transient porn sites. We've already had emails from a couple of readers who, in their excitement, registered without checking for contact details or a cancellation policy. If it's porn you want, you should be safe with some of the larger operations, but always check for a postal address, and find out what the procedure is for cancelling your account.

Joining the Playboy Online member's only section – **http://www.playboy.com** – will set you back $6.95 a month. Not bad for access to the online version of the world's most famous 'gentleman's' magazine. And there's so much more available to members than yet more explicit pictures – or so we're told.

If that isn't you thing, how about subscribing to the JenniCAM? At the bargain price of $12 a year, you get to join in with one of the Net's biggest events. JenniCAM Members

receive a new updated image every 2 minutes – rather than 20 – and there are additional viewing options to allow you to run JenniCAM in the background. See **http://www.jennicam.org**.

CHAPTER FIVE: SMALL BUSINESSES

CHAPTER 5

SMALL BUSINESSES

Small businesses are waking up to the potential of the Net, and beating the high street stores online. Paul Russell looks at why the little fish are taking the plunge

CHAPTER FIVE: SMALL BUSINESSES

So 1999 is supposed to be the year that e-commerce takes off. Hang on a minute, wasn't that also predicted at the beginning of last year? And the year before that? But now that fears about credit card fraud are on the decrease, we're all waking up to the idea of buying online. It should be cheaper, more convenient and quicker than real-life shopping. But take a stroll down your local high street. Chances are you'll find a Boots, a Marks and Spencer, and maybe a Gap. Now look up the sites on the Web. You'll find a good, professional site to advertise the store, but it's unlikely that you'll be able to buy anything from the comfort of your home. While the big stores are paying lip service to e-commerce, the market has been left wide open for small businesses and shopkeepers to take the plunge. If you go to an online UK shopping directory and visit the food category, you will find Tesco, but many other big names are conspicuous by their absence. But alongside Tesco, you'll find such obscure names as Jim Garrahy's Fudge Kitchen, Lossie Seafood and Macdonald's Smoked Produce, often small, family businesses in the sleepy backwaters of Britain. And while Tesco will only deliver to you if you live within driving distance of 12 selected stores, shops like Jack Scaife butchers will deliver their produce worldwide. Why is this? Well, it could be that local shops and small businesses have realised that they have so much more to gain. A chain like Sainsbury's or Tesco already has a presence all over the country, but for a small cost, a family business can go national and global.

Virtual stores

Of course, that's not to say that the only shops on the Net are local stores and family businesses. There are some fantastic money-raking success stories like Amazon, but these sites are usually purely virtual affairs – their success is down to the fact that they are freed from the expense of maintaining a bricks-and-mortar presence and so can offer lower prices than other high street stores.

CHAPTER FIVE: SMALL BUSINESSES

Adrian Merrick, the man behind the UK online shopping mall Enterprise City, which can be found at **http://www.enterprisecity.co.uk**, believes that e-commerce is taking off slowly, but what is holding it back is the poor choice of shops in many retail areas – people want to shop around and compare prices, but at present that just isn't possible. Although his mall aims to include all online UK shops and it offers free space to shops using a secure server, the site contains details of less than 400 shops.

In the absence of major competition, and the advent of relatively cheap software for setting up an online outlet, many small businesses have realised that getting their products online is a cheap and effective way to give the products national and worldwide coverage. And home delivery is something that small businesses know all about. As these operations are often isolated in local communities, they have long relied on mail order for a large amount of their business, usually advertised in traditional print media.

Bringing home the bacon

Take the example of Chris Battle, who runs the Yorkshire-based Jack Scaife butchers. Battle opened his Internet site for business at **http://www.classicengland.co.uk** two years ago. The family business consists of his wife Barbara, their two daughters, and 11 employees. Battle explains how the site came about.

"We did quite a lot of mail order and quite a lot of

CHAPTER FIVE: SMALL BUSINESSES

advertising to get that mail order business, through magazines and various regional and national papers. At the end of the year it was quite an expense. Then my daughters suggested the Internet, which was something I was sceptical about – I didn't think that the type of people that accessed the Internet were the type of people that would want to buy bacon, sausages and black pudding. But they talked me into it."

Before taking the plunge, the Battle family checked out the online competition and found that there wasn't any. During their research, they came across Paradigm Web solutions' Classic England shopping mall site at **http://www.classicengland.co.uk** and were impressed by what they saw. The mall showcases the online shops created by Paradigm, heavily featuring shops selling traditional English goods. Battle provided Paradigm with some photos of his family and staff, gave the designers a basic idea of what he wanted on the site, and let them get on with it. The Internet now accounts for 20 per cent of his turnover and this figure is increasing all the time. Battle paid Paradigm around £1,000 to set up and maintain the online shop for the first year, and he now pays £250 per year for the site's maintenance and update. It seems to be money well spent. "Before, we were spending between £4,000 and £5,000 on advertising, with a fraction of the audience... we're just a small family business, but we're as big as multinational and international companies. We've got the same footing, which is nice," says Battle.

No fear

If it costs so little to have a shopping site on the Net, why aren't more people doing it? Battle reckons most of them are frightened of the unknown, saying "I certainly would have been if it hadn't been for my daughters. I mean, I've only just got used to the

CHAPTER FIVE: SMALL BUSINESSES

calculator." After his initial scepticism about selling on the Net, he is very pleased with the results – turnover is increasing by £100,000 per year, "and a lot of that is to do with the Internet… it just shows how wrong I was. I've had to eat my bacon, as it were, I just got it totally wrong and I don't mind admitting it."

The Floyd Consultancy (**http://www.floyd.co.uk**) produces online shopping software aimed specifically at small businesses. It estimates that although most of its software is snapped up by Web developers like Paradigm, small businesses themselves account for 30 per cent of sales. Roger Biddle of Provender Delicatessen is one such example of the complete DIY shop builder.

Like Battle, Roger Biddle's deli in Somerset had been operating a successful mail order service. After dabbling in computers for several years, he felt confident enough to set up a site to give his shop front a national and international presence. He was determined to get noticed on the Net and joined a discussion group newsletter to learn how to market his site and get listed in search engines. He describes setting up the Wessex Provender site (**http://www.users.globalnet.co.uk/~proven/provender**) as costing a lot of time, but not that much money. He certainly seems to have got his site noticed – the Christmas 1998 online takings were four times that of Christmas 1997, and he now has 200 people on his mailing list. So where are the visitors to his site coming from? The shop's presence in UK shopping malls seems to be

CHAPTER FIVE: SMALL BUSINESSES

the crucial factor. Enterprise City and ShopGuide both provide an equally large amount of his traffic, much more than that generated by search engines. And with all the talk about the power of the Net, it's a sobering fact that a mention in the press caused the biggest surge of visitors to his online shop. After being baffled by an abnormally high number of hits, Biddle discovered that his online shop had just been mentioned in the national press.

Selling online seems to be a cheap, low risk way to bring in money. And as the real-life high street has been slow to fill the online shopping malls, tiny online shops have found it easy to get noticed by positioning themselves in these virtual outlets. Perhaps the only drawback for small businesses looking to trade in the online malls is that most charge rent for their space.

Space for rent

Adrian Merrick was interested in the success of rent-charging online malls like BarclaySquare at **http://www.barclaysquare.co.uk**, and was quick to recognise a gap in the market for a shopping mall that offered free space. With this in mind, last August he set up the Enterprise City shopping mall at **http://www.enterprisecity.co.uk**, and has been steadily building visitor rates ever since. Enterprise City is financed by banner advertising, and some stores are given an enhanced presence, for which Enterprise City takes a percentage of the store's profit. Merrick believes that as few as 10-20 per cent of big retailers are selling online, and that this lack of choice for consumers is holding back UK e-commerce. His views are backed up by Peter Hemsley, Sales and Marketing Director of the Floyd Consultancy, a company that sells the ShopAssistant software for small businesses. He feels that "e-commerce is taking off at a reasonable rate, given the number of shops that are available." Hemsley believes that if you

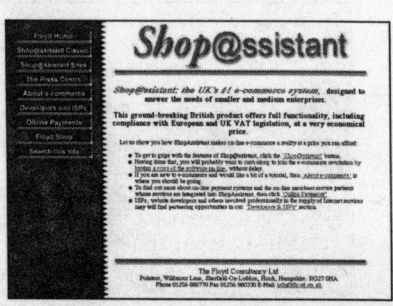

CHAPTER FIVE: SMALL BUSINESSES

define a shop as an online site that includes payment online, "there are probably only about 1,000 shops operational in the UK."

According to Merrick, the look and design of some sites lets them down. "If you think about it, the same sorts of things should apply on the Web as apply to the high street. If you were walking down the high street, you wouldn't go into a shop that was bland or dirty, where the staff were just sitting around and eating their food. And the same sort of thing applies to the Web – if you don't see a shop that inspires you to go into it, then you won't buy there. I think that store owners should look at their site from a stand-off perspective, and try to view it how a shopper would view it for the first time, as though it was a store in the high street."

Overall, Merrick feels that because the number of shops is now increasing, e-commerce is starting to take off, and he knows that when it does, he has a foot in the door. This view is shared by Hemsley, who says that sales of ShopAssistant are growing at 30 per cent per month, "and that is at least indicative of the rate at which smaller companies are getting themselves aligned behind e-commerce."

Some small businesses can find it hard to get a place in the market. Jonathan Hughes-Jones of Hereford-based Pembridge Terracotta makes hand-thrown terracotta pots and has six staff. Around 18 months ago he launched a Web site to sell his wares. The first version of the site was quite successful, despite not offering online payment, and got around 2,000 hits a month. The result? A few thousand pounds worth of orders for very little outlay or effort. Naturally, Hughes-Jones was

CHAPTER FIVE: SMALL BUSINESSES

impressed and decided to spend a bit more money on the site by including online ordering. The necessary software cost a few hundred pounds, and by the time he had paid a consultant to build the online shopping software into his site, the price tag had risen to around a £1,000. However, the new site at **http://www.pterra.demon.co.uk**, although almost identical to the first, now receives a fraction of the number of hits and sales of its predecessor. Hughes-Jones believes that the rapid decline in interest is because, unlike the previous site, the new URL is not listed in Yahoo!, despite his attempts to get it included. A frustrated Hughes-Jones knows that "99 per cent of people on the Net are never going to find us, unless we've told them through some other media." He describes the new level of sales as "pathetic. Having said that, one of them is a good American wholesaler, and that in itself may well justify the whole thing." Having now invested a fair amount of money in the project, Hughes-Jones is determined to achieve his original aim. "We want to sell retail to people all over the world. Basically, we want to cut out the middleman, and do what the Internet ought, in theory, be able to do. And we just got a taste of it the first time around, and thought 'it's going to work, this is easy, this is great,' and now it's all fallen down. We may just have to advertise like hell in other media. That's the conclusion we're fast coming to – that unless you're in Yahoo!, you have to spend a lot of money in other media."

Online catalogues

While Hughes-Jones is considering advertising his online shop outside the confines of the Web, many small businesses that have previously relied on printed catalogues to sell their goods, are realising that online selling can do the same job at a fraction of the cost.

CHAPTER FIVE: SMALL BUSINESSES

Jim Oldroyd of Last Chance Books in Sevenoaks, Kent, used to print four or five catalogues a year for his trade customers – catalogues he described as being out of date almost as soon as they were printed. Now, his catalogue is on the Web at **http://www.oldroyd.co.uk** at a fraction of the cost.

The CookCraft site (**http://www.cookcraft.com**) was launched by Richard Stell 18 months ago, with Stell coding the HTML himself. He saw it as a way to avoid the cost of printing thousands of catalogues of kitchen equipment and, of course, to open up new markets. The worldwide exposure has thrown up a few surprises – a piece of terracotta pottery that he thought would be a dead loss is proving a big hit with overseas buyers (perhaps Pembridge Terracotta should get in touch). He admits that if this was a conventional business, it wouldn't be doing well. But as overheads are minimal, things are going well. At a conservative estimate, business is doubling every four to five months. and the more stock he puts on the site, the more business increases. At the moment the site is not his main business – like Adrian Merrick at Enterprise City, Stell intends the site to be his foot in the door for when UK Internet shopping really takes off. He's found it a steep learning curve with instant feedback – if he changes the site, he can monitor the results as the number of hits, and also see which pages are most popular. And now is the time to make mistakes. When he wiped out his site for a few days with an over-ambitious piece of Java, he lost modest takings. If the site takes off as he hopes, then in a few years' time a mistake like that would be a catastrophe. A case of growing up in public.

So, there are plenty of online success stories from small businesses, and these can be attributed to several factors – familiarity with mail order, the availability of cheap software to run commercial Web sites, and the lack of competition from high street stores.

And, of course, the fact that a local business has so much more to gain by 'going national' than a large multinational which already has a presence in every town.

While the major stores are testing the waters and sitting in marketing meetings, the nation's shopkeepers and entrepreneurs have got stuck in. How they will fare when the big corporates finally decide to move in is a matter for speculation, but it seems certain that by getting there first, some will be doing very nicely.

CHAPTER FIVE: SMALL BUSINESSES

THE VIRTUAL HIGH STREET

Enterprise City
http://www.enterprisecity.co.uk

A friendly-looking mall that includes over 350 online shops, all offering online selling via a secure server

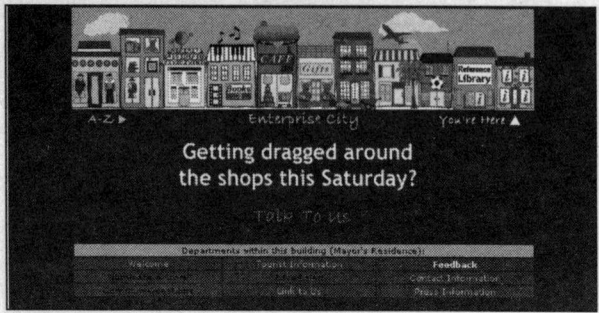

Classic England
http://www.classicengland.co.uk

A Web site hosted by Paradigm Web Solutions. The focus is on traditional, small British businesses

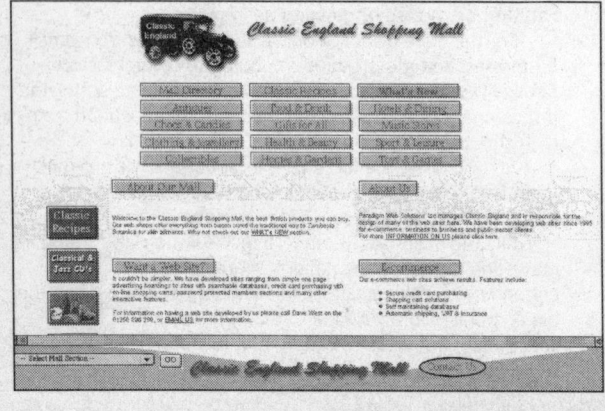

CHAPTER FIVE: SMALL BUSINESSES

ShopGuide
http://www.shopguide.co.uk
Links and reviews to over 300 secure online shops. Shops are listed in order of their ShopGuide rating

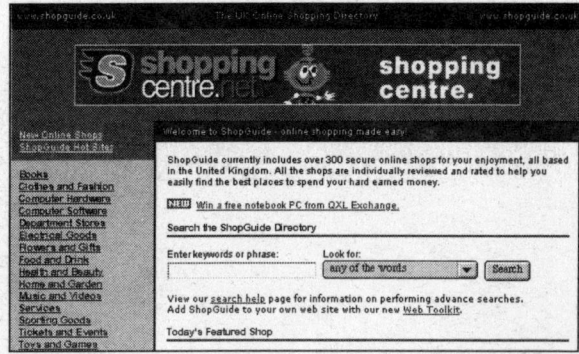

UK Shopping City
http://www.ukshops.co.uk
Part high street, part industrial estate

CHAPTER SIX: PASSION FOR FASHION

A PASSION FOR FASHION

It started with music and books, but now clothes shops are turning to e-commerce for revenue. Jo Chipchase takes a look at the fashion industry's foray on to the virtual high street

CHAPTER SIX: PASSION FOR FASHION

Unless you're a sucker for punishment, you don't need to fight your way along a busy high street to buy your jeans and jackets. Instead, you can avoid the traumas and the sore feet, as online versions of your favourite shopping emporiums are available via the Web, 24-hours a day, seven days a week.

By the year 2003, the UK online retail market is forecast to be worth £3 billion. Of this total, the clothing market will account for £405 million, making it the third largest sector, behind computers and flights. Blazing the online retail trail started in other sectors by the likes of Amazon, the rag trade is dipping into the lucrative waters of the Net. The rush to set up cyberstores is driven, in part, by decreasing consumer anxiety about the security of online transactions. Some fashion retailers are receiving demands from customers to provide their garments online, and with the emergence of free ISPs such as Freeserve, the Internet is becoming ever more prevalent in British homes.

Into virgin territory

Unsurprisingly in view of its advertising spend, Levi Strauss at **http://www.levi.com** was one of the first fashion retailers to set up on the Web. Diesel was also ahead of the field – initially going live in 1995 – and now with wacky and well-designed online stores at **http://www.diesel.com** and **http://www.diesel.co.uk**. Not far behind was Paul Smith, whose original site went live during 1996. The current site at **http://www.paulsmith.co.uk**, up since last October, attracts 42,000 page impressions a month. "There is potential to sell to a global market. Most of our visitors are from the US and Japan, with the UK coming third. They appreciate the Britishness of the Paul Smith brand," explains Richard Quance of Foresight New Media, the project manager for the Paul Smith site.

They also appreciate the size of the profits to be made. In the US, the Gap site at **http://www.gap.com** took over $1 million in revenue from online sales during 1998,

CHAPTER SIX: PASSION FOR FASHION

which is roughly equivalent to Gap's second most profitable US store – but without the high fixed costs associated with running a retail outlet. With this sort of money to be made, fashion labels and their watered-down high street counterparts will fight for the attention of online consumers.

And vice versa. Bob Shevlin, director of new media at Diesel, says, "I wish we could say we have always been great Internet visionaries in Diesel, but the answer for our getting involved in e-commerce quite early has had more to do with who our customers are than who we are. Diesel customers are early adopters – the kind of people who are completely unafraid of new developments, such as online shopping. Our customers have basically demanded online shopping. We've simply responded to this interest." However, online fashion retailing is still at a relatively immature stage. Well known fashion houses Prada and Gucci both have sites 'coming soon' at http://www.prada.com and http://www.gucci.com. Certain labels, including Dexter Wong and the trendy new Japanese brand Superlovers, have registered domain names and are using them for email, but are currently without Web sites. And many well known labels will soon be playing catch-up.

From Gucci to Great Universal

So what fashion items are we buying via the Net? According to Martin Reeves, the man behind the ShopGuide retail search engine at **http://www.shopguide.co.uk**, people go for established brands. The Great Universal catalogue brands, such as Kays at **http://www.kaysnet.com**, are particularly popular and 'lingerie' is the keyword most frequently entered into the ShopGuide search engine. "People go for established brands because of consumer confidence," Reeves explains. "If people have been shopping with Kays, it's a natural progression. Catalogue-based outlets have the infrastructure in place and people tend to have confidence in their service policies."

CHAPTER SIX: PASSION FOR FASHION

Despite their tendency to splash out using plastic cards in shops, people may be more conservative when buying online. This could be bad news for high-end fashion retailers that sell expensive goods. "We've only ever seen one single order over £1,000," says Reeves, "and just a few over £500." The logical explanation is that some (cheaper) items are inherently suited to online selling – after all, the fit of a pair of pants is less critical than the fit of a designer jacket. Not to mention less painful on the pocket if you decide your purchase was a mistake. Richard Quance believes the problem lies in knowing how a garment will look on you. "The Web is ideal for accessories, underwear, T-shirts and jeans, but less good for selling expensive items where people want to know how it will fit."

Whether or not a site is successful in selling fashion items depends partly on its design. Just as the interior and layout of 'real' shops varies vastly, the same is true of online retail sites. While some opt for a simple 'clothes only' approach – such as Gap – others provide a plethora of content that makes the clothes seem almost incidental. The Red or Dead site at **http://www.redordead.co.uk** is a prime example of this approach, featuring all sorts of zany content, based on Flash and with a multitude of windows that pop up everywhere. The clothes are restricted to three brief catwalk 'movies' from Salt Lake City, Seattle or Miami. You're more likely to find yourself

CHAPTER SIX: PASSION FOR FASHION

looking at the 'Red or Dead love story,' or the 'Wayne's World' section complete with strange 'cold dips and hot tips.' But what if you just want their garments and footwear?

Many fashion sites make a clear attempt to combine retail and e-zine content to gain repeat visits. The Arcadia and Burton Group sites – which include familiar high street names such as Top Shop at **http://www.tops.co.uk**, Dorothy Perkins at **http://www.dorothyperkins.co.uk** and Burtons at **http://www.burton menswear.co.uk** – back up the clothes with competitions, club guides, and other magazine-type features. Taking a slightly different approach, the site of street/clubwear label Firetrap at **http://www.firetrap.co.uk** could easily fool you into thinking it belongs to an online publication or an advertising agency. There are no clothes for sale on the site, but you will find content that pokes fun at New Lads, including a spoof study of asylum patients – inmates include 'Kylie Muff' – aka Kylie Minogue. The site has a recruitment section and press releases, which is less than helpful if you want to buy a jacket. It also showcases Firetrap's risqué publicity ads, which are worth a peek.

So does this extraneous content actually work? Richard Quance thinks it can. "People like to be entertained and to feel as if they've had an exciting experience. Additional content lodges things in people's brains." However, he is adverse to overly flashy sites. "If people get confused because a site is too complex, they'll leave very quickly – as they would do in a real shop." Martin Reeves agrees. "The clothing catalogue is the most important thing. Webzine content is part of the strategy

CHAPTER SIX: PASSION FOR FASHION

to encourage repeat visits and send visitors off to different areas of the online catalogue. A major design fault is to have too many peripheral things that don't enhance the shopping experience."

Are you being served?

When shopping on the high street, you wouldn't expect to encounter rude assistants in stores, and then put up with shoddy goods, or buy items that are not covered by exchange or return policies. The same applies to online shopping. A good online retail site should have a clearly stated policy for delivery, customer service and returns. The company behind the site should make their identity and contact details clear. As with offline shopping, it's unwise to buy an expensive item that may need to be returned if you don't know who you're buying it from.

Diesel's Bob Shevlin emphasises the need for online customer care. "Customer service infrastructure is the one under-developed element, I believe, in many new online commerce ventures. Online shoppers who shop with established brands are much less concerned about security than they are with customer service. You must be available to respond when issues arise. For example, it is a statistical probability that there will be delivery issues with a certain small percentage of customers. These people will want an immediate personal follow-up from your company when this occurs, and you must be able to give it to them, seven days a week, or you shouldn't be selling online."

Martin Reeves at ShopGuide emphasises that his company will be focusing on consumer advice and returns. Michael Hammond of Axfords points out that failing to respond promptly to emails from customers within 24-hours is unacceptable. Bob Shevlin agrees: "From the very beginning, we've replied personally to all email that we receive. This is enormously time-consuming, but is crucial to preserving our loyal consumers' traffic to our Web site. You simply can't invite customers into your Web pages, offer them an email link, and then ignore or execute an auto-response to the messages they send you."

The future

Although the online fashion industry is not yet mature, it may only be a matter of time before it is commonplace to cyber shop for most of our wardrobes. Bob Shevlin says that "Fashion is

CHAPTER SIX: PASSION FOR FASHION

under-represented online right now, because many brands worry that they will have difficulty translating their image though their Web sites. This will change in the near future, and higher-end fashion brands will begin piling on to the Web because it's too powerful a communications medium to ignore." But what will be their market share? If some research statistics are to be believed, catalogue-based operations operating at the lower end of the market, such as Great Universal, will be the big players on the virtual high street.

Richard Quance predicts that the larger retailers will see the potential of online shopping, and the wide audience, willing to buy. "However, it is vital to have the right support – customer care and fast delivery – and to meet people's expectations. There is no reason why it can't become a big market, but it must be done with care," he says.

If you haven't yet given your credit card a little exercise on the Internet, why not start with one of the sites we've covered here? Perhaps a pair of boxers from Kiniki, or a T-shirt from Diesel. Once you've started, you may never want to brave the high street stores again.

FETISH FAYRE

One area of the fashion industry that takes well to the Net is

CHAPTER SIX: PASSION FOR FASHION

fetish wear. Whether you want to flirt with tight-fitting PVC, or you're a serious S&M-er, there's something to make your credit card (or other things) twitch. A good starting point is Skin Two's easy-to-navigate online offering at **http://www.skintwo.co.uk/clothing**. Here, you'll find two catalogues with designs for men and women. Interesting items include a PVC suspender belt and stockings for her, or a pair of chaps for him.

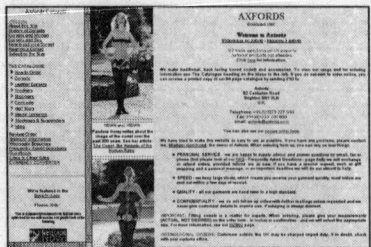

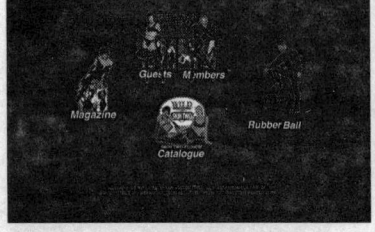

A vast range of fetish clothing, including the Skin Two collection and the popular Wild Designs catalogue, is available at the nicely-designed **http://www.fetish.co.uk site**. According to John Gilson of Bookstore, who maintains the site, it attracts between one and two million hits a month. No mean figure for something that has been online for just six months. The site is currently being redesigned to include a shopping basket facility and 'Hawte' software that monitors and certifies users to ensure they're who they appear to be. Gilson stresses that it is important to verify security, from the point of view of vendor and buyer alike. He also emphasises the need to provide supporting content, rather than just the clothes. "The normal way people approach fetish clothing, if they don't know much about it, is that they want to get something at a fair price. On fetish sites, clothing care information and details of club events are important."

Gilson's view is shared by Michael Hammond of Brighton-based fine corsetry maker, Axfords, at **http://www.axfords.com**. The Axford site sells a wide range of items – the most popular one being a simple, black satin corset. "We provide information on the history of corsets and how they are fitted," says Hammond. "If people know the sizes, the advantage is the immediacy of it –

CHAPTER SIX: PASSION FOR FASHION

you can buy something on a Sunday morning." He says that the best-selling items tend to be ones that will easily fit.

Is there any clear difference between fashion retail online and fetish fashion retail online? No – but Hammond says that hit rates may be higher, because of Internet users' propensity to seek sex-related content. "Fetish wear places more of a strain on bandwidth than normal fashion."

SOURCES AND STARTING POINTS

alt.fashion
A good place to discuss the latest lippy, darling

alt.sex.fetish.fashion
A good place to discuss the latest rubber trousers

http://www.fashionangel.comangel.html
The Angel of Fashion Award – a useful directory of fashion on the Web

http://www.widemedia.com/fashionuk
FashionUK – fashion zine from the streets of London

http://www.hypermode.com
Deluxe US fashion zine

http://www.lumiere.com
Fashion magazine based in Paris and New York

http://www.vogue.co.uk
Conde Naste's big selling UK fashion mag online

WHERE TO GET...

...T-shirts, jeans, jackets, dresses
Take a trip to the UK-dedicated Diesel site at **http://www.diesel.co.uk**. It offers a comprehensive range of

CHAPTER SIX: PASSION FOR FASHION

jeans, jackets, dresses, T-shirts and bags. While you browse, you can listen to background 'musick', with tunes such as 'Perusal Palpitations' and 'Happy Shoppa Bossa.' The site has a customer service section and a 'speed shop' (no – it's not what you might be thinking), which contains just the key items from the Diesel collection.

The Levi's site (**http://www.levi.com**, with European option) offers the selection of jeans you would expect. Navigation is straightforward, which means it is easy to find the clothes. You can chat to other site users while browsing – what you say appears in a band at the top of the site's main frame. If you get bored with shopping, you can always play a Shockwave game (something to do with finding lost denim) or view a selection of Real Media clips.

...A variety of predictable items

La Redoute, at **http://www.redoute.co.uk**, offers 'French fashion for all the family,' with 15 per cent discount on Internet orders. You can search through men's and women's collections and buy the items online. Menswear includes a Joseph padded jacket for £150, parkas, jeans and more. The site also offers a range of underwear, including Calvin Klein boxers, and shoes courtesy of Caterpillar and other known brands.

...Underwear

It's underwear for him at the Kiniki Direct Male site (**http://www.kiniki.com**), which now has 'larger and more detailed pictures' of thongs, briefs and swimwear. Blimey! Moving swiftly to undies for her at Caroline B Lingerie. At **http://www.caroline-b.com/lingerie.htm** you can buy lingerie of the tasteful variety from three different catalogues, and stockings, too. The haute couture lingerie from Paris is rather impressive.

...Footwear

The ideal destination for those who enjoy (a) oversized platform footwear or (b) resembling a Spice Girl circa 1997 is Buffalo Boots, at **http://www.buffalo-boots.com**. The company provides a nicely designed site. Besides buying boots, you can download a screensaver while you're there.

Shoeworld claims to be Europe's biggest footwear site. Online at **http://www.shoeworld.com**, it has a footwear glossary and

CHAPTER SIX: PASSION FOR FASHION

links to a wealth of sites belonging to well-known footwear retailers. A good starting point.

...Bored

On Next's site, at **http://www.next.co.uk**, you can order a hard copy of the Next directory and browse Next's Autumn/Winter 98 collection (sooo timely, darling), which features pictures of rather bored-looking people modelling various garments. In case you're interested in a retail career, there's information on job opportunities at Next. Not the most exciting of fashion sites, but tipped by at least one research agency as a likely success story.

John Smedley's site, at **http://www.john-smedley.co.uk**, is the place to browse items made from high quality yarns and read information about yarn spinning. You'll also learn that the company supplies M&S. How exciting.

VEXED GENERATION

A company that uses additional content to its advantage is Vexed Generation, a London-based fashion house supplying streetwear, at **http://www.vexed.co.uk**. The Vexed Generation site favours chaotic animations and radar-style graphics and confronts visitors with stark urban issues – such as privacy and surveillance, personal security, pollution and police powers. According to Rob Smith of Omniscience, the agency responsible for the site, the philosophy displayed online fits with the splash-proofed, advanced material of Vexed Generation's clothing. "The site is built to have a different focus to most fashion offerings. Although Vexed Generation make clothes, they have a vast ideology and belief system, and the site puts

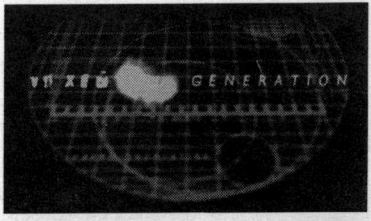

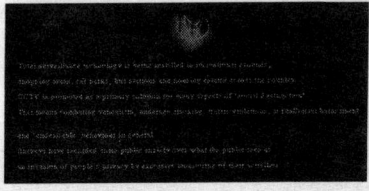

CHAPTER SIX: PASSION FOR FASHION

across the issues on which their garments are based." Although site visitors can go straight to the clothes, they also have the option of navigating the 'Information Terrorist' – a clever back-end that uses agent-based techniques to assess whether people are interested in what it has to say. Server and client-side calculations are used to monitor and react to visitors' interaction with the content. Folk who simply click through quickly without absorbing the information will find that they don't get very far. Smith explains: "The Information Terrorist monitors how long you spend reading the information and what options you choose. The text darkens if you're not interested and penalties are incurred. Eventually, it will kick you out if you just click through. It is a good means of showing that some sites are compiling information on you. We've had a lot of media attention. Information Terrorist is a good way of supporting the clothes." The approach has proved successful for Vexed Generation, and the site accounts for 20 per cent of turnover. The other 80 per cent of sales are made through the company's one retail outlet in London. "The site gives Vexed Generation the ability to raise awareness and reach a wide audience," says Smith. "We have received responses from all around the world."

CHAPTER SIX: PASSION FOR FASHION

A-Z OF SHOPPING SITES

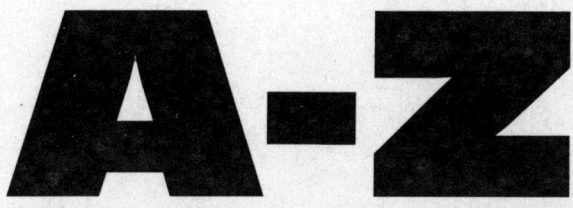

OF SHOPPING SITES

By now you should have some idea of how online shopping works, and what kinds of benefits it can offer. So now it's time to buy something! What follows is an A-Z of the best shopping sites on the Web

A-Z OF SHOPPING SITES

A-Z OF SHOPPING SITES

Action Computers
http://www.action.com/

A nifty site that not only sells computers, but which also sells peripherals, software and even office stationary. Once you've decide what you want, you'll even be told of how much you have saved by shopping online.

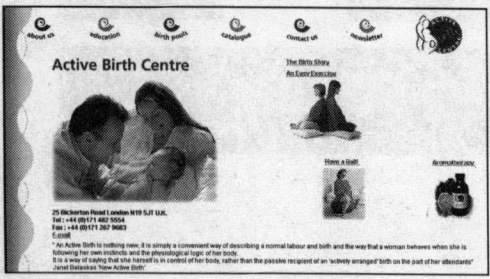

Active Birth Centre
http://www.activebirthcentre.com/

If you, or someone you know is pregnant, you can find loads of gifts and goodies that will please both mother and child.

A-Z OF SHOPPING SITES

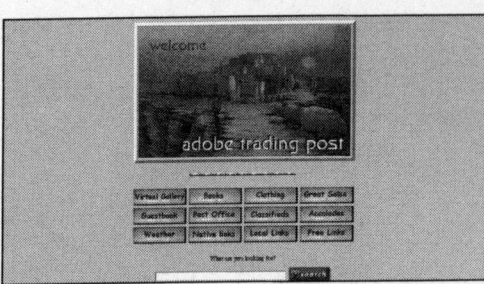

Adobe Trading Post
http://www.powerplace.com/

The place to come if you're interested in Native American art and clothes. Expect lots of turquoise and airbrushed denim.

alphabet street
http://www.alphabetstreet.infront.co.uk/

An excellent online bookshop that has some real bargains. When we visited you could buy bestsellers at a 50 per cent discount. Can't say fairer than that.

A-Z OF SHOPPING SITES

The Amazing Interactive T-Shirt Company
http://www.jerseyvirtual.net/shirts/

If you see a Web site that has graphics to die for, visit this site and get the image put in a t-shirt or jumper.

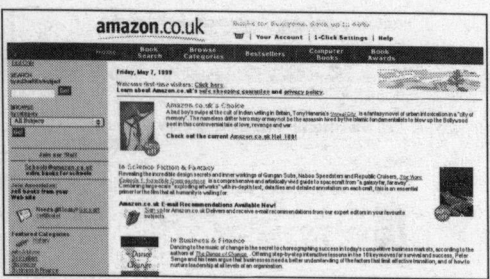

Amazon
http://www.amazon.co.uk

The UK version of the excellent Amazon.com service, if you want a book, you can be pretty sure that you'll find it here.

A-Z OF SHOPPING SITES

Animail
http://www.animail.co.uk/

Don't forget about your animal friends when you go shopping – visit Animail for loads of goodies for creatures great and small.

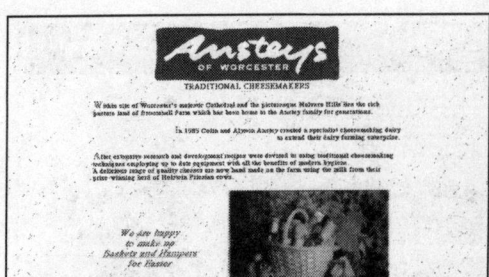

Ansteys of Worcester
http://www.foodhall.co.uk/ansteys-cheese

This company has its own herd of cows, so you can be assured that the cheese you buy from there is nice and fresh. As a bonus, all cheeses are free from rennet, so vegetarians can buy what they like.

A-Z OF SHOPPING SITES

Apple UK and Ireland
http://www.uk.euro.apple.com/cgibin/
WebObjects/Apple

For all you Mac lovers out there, the mothership is here. Visit the Apple store to stock up on all your latest goodies.

Archie McPhee
http://www.mcphee.com/

Lots of weird gifts that will appeal to all with a love for kitsch retro booty.

A-Z OF SHOPPING SITES

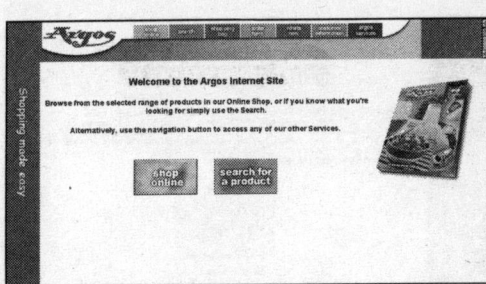

Argos
http://www.argos.co.uk

Argos already makes shopping easier, and now you don't even have to leave your house to stock up on goods.

Aroma Theraputics
http://www.internetshopping.com/
default.asp?goto=/Aromatherapy/Aroma1.asp

Everybody needs something to help them relax, and one of the legal options is aromatherapy. Visit this site and you could be filling your days with beneficial smells.

A-Z OF SHOPPING SITES

Arts and Crafts Internet Mall

http://www.artcraftmall.com/

A US-based site full of crafts. Some of it is pretty ropey, but hunt around and you'll find some real treasures.

Artstream

http://www.artstream.com

If you like your arts and crafts, you'll like Artstream as it sells all manner of artistic goodies. There's sculpture, paintings, drawings – even digital masterpieces.

A-Z OF SHOPPING SITES

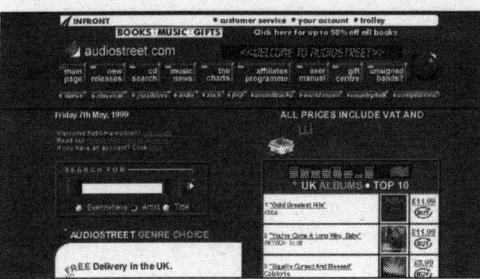

Audiostreet
http://www.audiostreet.infront.co.uk

You're not going to save a huge amount on your CDs with Audiostreet, but with free pack and postage on all orders in the UK, it will save a trip to the shops.

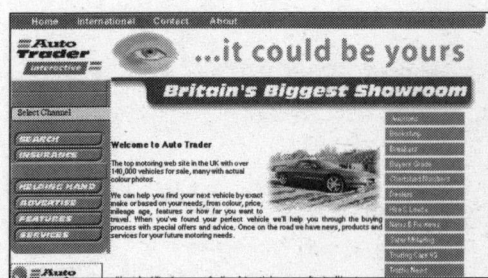

Auto Trader Interactive
http://www.autotrader.co.uk/

The well-known magazine peddling used cars is online for you to browse through. There's colour pictures to accompany each car, so you know exactly what you're getting.

A-Z OF SHOPPING SITES

B

A-Z OF SHOPPING SITES

Bargain Holidays
http://www.bargainholidays.com/

This huge site is continually updated so you get the very latest information about tempting deals that will whisk you away to some tropical climate.

Barnes and Noble
http://www.barnesandnoble.com

Beginning with the bold statement that "If we don't have your book, nobody does," Barnes and Noble is indeed a very good site.

A-Z OF SHOPPING SITES

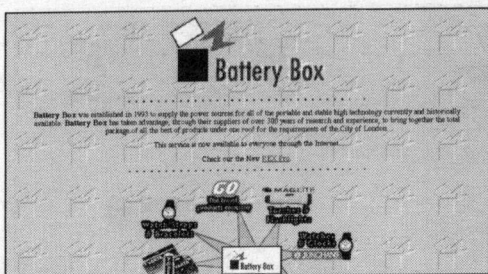

The Battery Box Web Site
http://www.battery-box.co.uk/

If you're forever running out of batteries, this site will solve your problem with its vast range of batteries. You can buy anything from watch batteries to power sticks for your walkman.

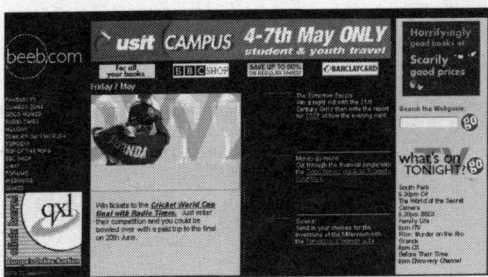

BBC Shop
http://www.bbcshop.com

This is the easiest way that you can get your hands on some great BBC products, whether you're a fan of *Only Fools and Horses*, or *Star Trek*.

A-Z OF SHOPPING SITES

Beers Direct
http://www.beersdirect.com/

If you like your drink to be of the yellow, fizzy persuasion, then stumble along to Beers Direct, for next day delivery of many beers.

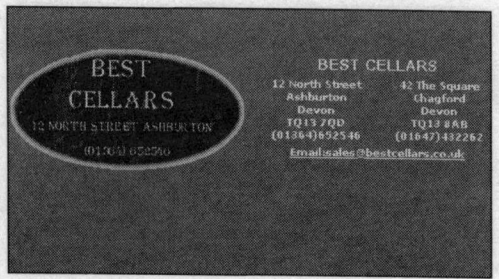

Best Cellars
http://www.devon.directory.co.uk/bestcellars/

For those with refined taste in wine, visit Best Cellars. As the name would suggest, the site offers a choice of the best wines from around the world.

A-Z OF SHOPPING SITES

BidnBuy

http://www.bidnbuy.com

Pretty self explanatory, you bid for whichever computer product you want, and then if your bid is successful, you can buy it.

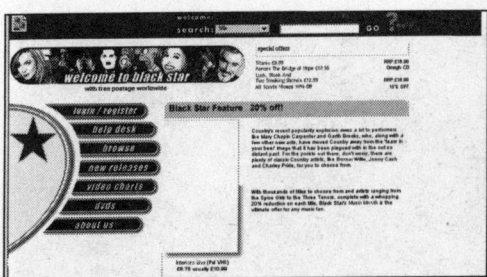

Black Star

http://www.blackstar.co.uk

You can stock up on all the latest videos from Black Star, and with free worldwide postage, you're going to make some savings, too.

A-Z OF SHOPPING SITES

B

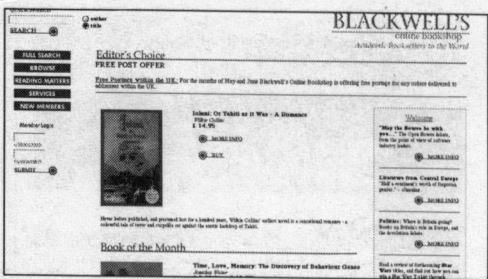

Blackwells
http://bookshop.blackwell.co.uk/

Academic booksellers to the world, Blackwells is the place to find all the books that will let you muse and ruminate on high brow issues.

The Body Shop
http://www.the-body-shop.com/

For those times when you want a bit of pampering, The Body Shop is an excellent source of gorgeous lotions and potions.

A-Z OF SHOPPING SITES

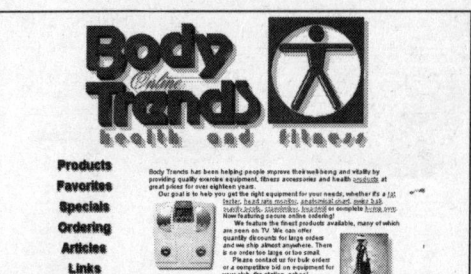

Body Trends
http://www.bodytrends.com/

Pump that body and give those muscles a work out with all the fitness products you can buy at Body Trends.

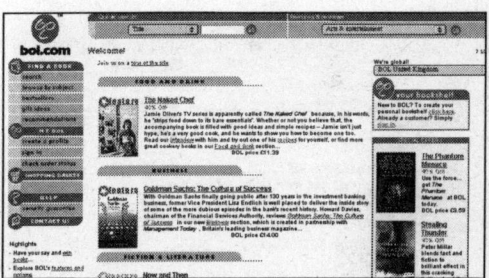

bol.com
http://www.uk.bol.com

A new Internet bookshop, that has loads of offers to whet the appetite. In addition to all the books, there are interviews with authors and loads of gift ideas.

A-Z OF SHOPPING SITES

Books.com
http://www.books.com

A very understated site from the States, where you may just find something that you can't get over in this country.

Borders
http://www.borders.com/

Search the online database of this excellent site for over 10 million books, CDs and videos. If you've ever been to the London store, you know what to expect.

A-Z OF SHOPPING SITES

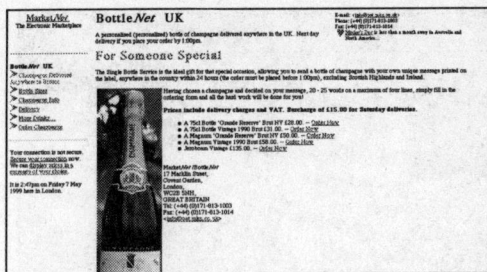

BottleNet
http://orders.mkn.co.uk/bottle/.en

Make someone's day by sending them a personalised bottle of champagne, complete with a 20-25 word message.

Boxman
http://www.boxman.co.uk/

A really impressive site for CDs. We managed to find a few titles that are normally only available in America, and the postage is cheap, too.

A-Z OF SHOPPING SITES

Bras Direct
http://www.brasdirect.co.uk/bras/default.asp

Whatever your shape or size, Bras Direct can give you the support you need with bras from a number of different manufacturers.

BT Shop
http://www.btshop.bt.com/

Get yourself connected with your friends near and far by buying yourself a phone.

A-Z OF SHOPPING SITES

Budget Rent a Car
http://www.budgetrentacar.com/home.html

This company offers a worldwide car hiring service, so book your car before you venture into foreign climes.

Bygone Era
http://www.bygone-era.co.uk

If you have a passion for classic or sports cars, you're going to need the clobber to go with it. Bygone Era supplies all the vintage-type clothes you need.

A-Z OF SHOPPING SITES

A-Z OF SHOPPING SITES

Campus Direct
http://www.usitcampus.com

If you're a student and you need somewhere to go on the cheap, visit this site for some cheap travel ideas to get away from studying.

Castle Search
http://www.castle-search.co.uk

House-hunting is one of the most tedious activities, but sites like Castle Search aim to make the whole process of renting or buying a property, a lot easier.

A-Z OF SHOPPING SITES

CDnow

http://www.cdnow.com

With CDnow, you get an excellent site selling a wide range of music. Whatever you want, you can be pretty sure that it's here, and the postage rates aren't extortionate, either.

The CD-ROM shop

http://www.cdimports.com

You can pick up some great discounts on CD-ROMS from this site, from a range that covers more than 31 categories.

A-Z OF SHOPPING SITES

Clothing Connection
http://www.clothingconnection.co.uk/

Get your discounted designer clothes from this site. You can pick up names such as Caterpiller, Kickers and French Connection and a snip of a price.

Computer Warehouse
http://www.cwonline.co.uk/start.html

You can snap up loads of computer goodies here, and make some real savings to boot.

A-Z OF SHOPPING SITES

Condomania
http://www.condoms4u.com/

Let Clever Dick guide you around this colourful site where you can buy condoms in all shapes, sizes, flavours, textures…

The Cooks Kitchen
http://www.kitchenware.co.uk/

Whatever your culinary prowess, it can always be improved, or at least made easier, by some decent utensils. Order your brand name kitchenware from this site.

A-Z OF SHOPPING SITES

Craft and Design London
http://craftdesign-london.com/

If you like your furniture like you like your designers – young and contemporary – get yourself along to here and deck out your abode in style.

Cricket Direct
http://www.cricketdirect.co.uk

Whether it's new balls you need, Cricket Direct stocks all the cricket bits and bobs you could possibly want. Howzat!

A-Z OF SHOPPING SITES

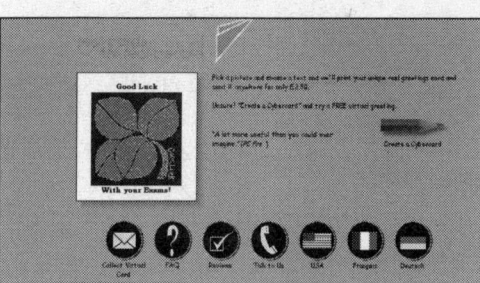

Cybercard
http://www.cybercard.co.uk/

Just can't find the right card for that special occasion? Visit Cybercard, and for £2.50, the company will send your personalised card anywhere.

Cyber-Ireland
http://homepage.tinet.ie/~dblack/cybereirinn/

For those with a penchant for the Emerald Isle, Cyber-Ireland lets you book holidays, and buy loads of Irish trinkets online.

A-Z OF SHOPPING SITES

A-Z OF SHOPPING SITES

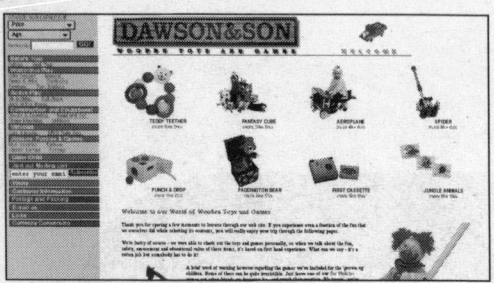

Dawson & Son
http://www.dawson-and-son.com

For a more traditional twist on toys that don't rely on flashy lights and electronic sounds, visit Dawsons & Sons for some quality wooden toys and games.

Dell UK
http://www.euro.dell.com

Nothing to do with Only Fools and Horses, Dell UK is an excellent site where you can buy a brand new computer.

A-Z OF SHOPPING SITES

Designers Direct
http://www.DesignersDirect.com/

Fancy swanning around in Kangol, Levis or maybe Clavin Klein? You can do just that thanks to this US site which has some tempting bargains, even after adding shipping costs

Diesel UK
http://ukstore.diesel.com/

Buy some cool clothes from the Diesel Web site, where you can have a gander at all the groovy gear on offer.

A-Z OF SHOPPING SITES

Digital Choice
http://www.digitalchoice.co.uk

All manners of digital tastes are catered for on this site, from TVs to videos to cameras and Hi-Fi's.

Disney Shopping
http://disney.go.com/shopping

Pick up all the latest in Disney goodies, whether it's clothes, collectibles or toys, you'll find it all here.

A-Z OF SHOPPING SITES

Dixons
http://www.dixons.co.uk

Enter the Dixons online superstore and purchase your goods from a range of TV's, videos and stereos

DiyTools
http://diytools.com

Tackle household nooks and crannies with some decent powertools, all of which you can pick up at this site.

A-Z OF SHOPPING SITES

Dorothy Perkins
http://www.dorothyperkins.co.uk

You can buy some great clothes from this site, and as it's part of the same group as Top Shop, Evans and Racing Green, you can scoot straight to them, too.

Drinks Direct
http://www.drinks-direct.co.uk

Order a wide range of sumptuous offerings from this site. The range not only includes drinks, but extends to hampers, flowers and chocolates.

A-Z OF SHOPPING SITES

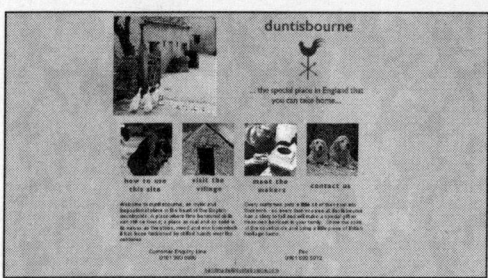

Duntisbourne
http://www.duntisbourne.com

Buy yourself a bit of Olde England with this site dealing in traditional hand-crafted goods. Buy something and then feel the quality.

DVD Express
http://www8.dvdexpress.com/consumer

If you've been seduced by the DVD 'revolution,' you can pick up some real bargains from this site. When we visited, there was 40 per cent off *Amistad* and *You've Got Mail*.

A-Z OF SHOPPING SITES

E

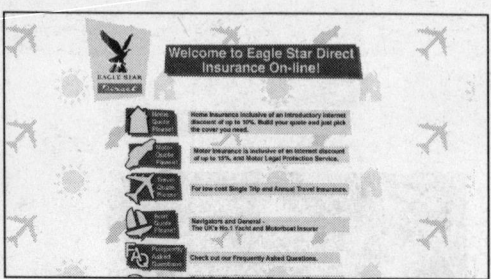

Eagle Star Direct
http://www.eaglestardirect.co.uk

Insurance may not be the most exciting thing to buy, but unfortunately, it's essential. This site is extremely user-friendly, and is well worth a look.

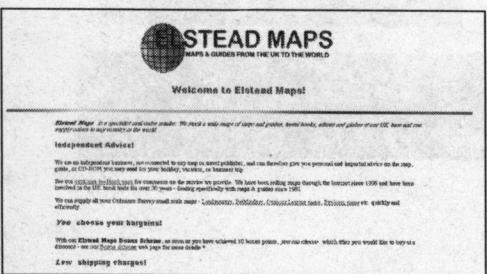

Elstead Maps
http://www.elstead.co.uk

Never be at a loss for where you are, with this site full of maps and navigation tools, you'll never lose direction again.

A-Z OF SHOPPING SITES

Entertainment Express
http://www.entexpress.com

Loads of entertainment goodies from video to music to multimedia. When we visited, the deals included *Mars Attack* for £3.99.

Eureka Records
http://home.clara.net/eureka

Viva la vinyl! This site stocks over 22,000 titles on that depleting medium. If you love your records, make sure you visit the site.

A-Z OF SHOPPING SITES

A-Z OF SHOPPING SITES

Fashion Direct
http://parasol.superx.net/fashion/

Get your smalls sorted out, visit this site and have all your lingerie needs seen to. There's undergarments for men and women.

Flowers Direct
http://www.flowersdirectuk.co.uk

For a beautiful display of blooms that will do anyone proud, Flowers Direct can come up with the bouquet, whatever the occasion.

A-Z OF SHOPPING SITES

Fortnum & Mason
http://fortnumandmason.co.uk

For some top notch fodder, come to this site of swanky London store, Fortnum and Mason. It's ever so refined, darling.

Futon Direct
http://www.futondirect.co.uk/

Funkier than sofas, futons offer very good value for money, especially with this site, which at the time of writing, was offering a further 15 per cent off the already reasonable prices

A-Z OF SHOPPING SITES

A-Z OF SHOPPING SITES

A-Z OF SHOPPING SITES

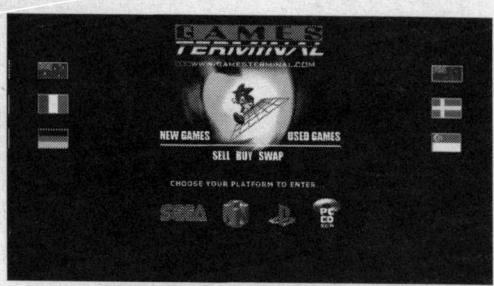

Games Terminal
http://www.gamesterminal.com/

An excellent site that lets you swap all your old games online. Simply pay the five pound fee, and you'll be engrossed in a new game in no time.

GB Posters
http://www.gbposters.co.uk/

If you love B-movies, you'll love this site, as within its collection of movie and music posters, you'll find an excellent selection of aliens and monsters.

A-Z OF SHOPPING SITES

Granada
http://www.granadahome.co.uk

A very foxy site for what is, essentially, some boxes with wires. You can buy all your home entertainment system here, as well as stuff for your kitchen.

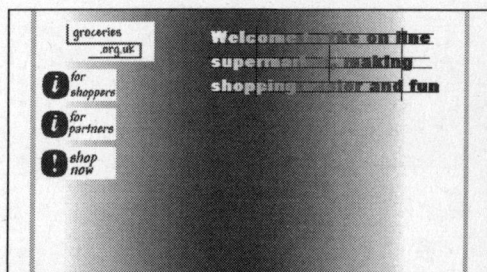

Groceries.org
http://www.Groceries.org.uk/

For those times when you just can't be bothered to go to the shops to buy your food, you can come here and stock up on the essentials.

A-Z OF SHOPPING SITES

A-Z OF SHOPPING SITES

H

Harts of Stur
http://www.harts-of-stur.co.uk

You can find lots of lovely shiny stainless steel on this site, which sells Stellar cookware. A must for professional and amateur cooks.

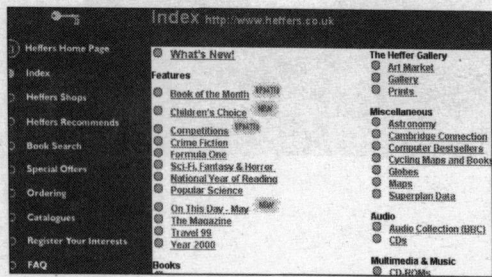

Heffers
http://www.heffers.co.uk

A huge site where you can buy books, multimedia CD-ROMs, maps, globes and even the odd pen and pencil.

A-Z OF SHOPPING SITES

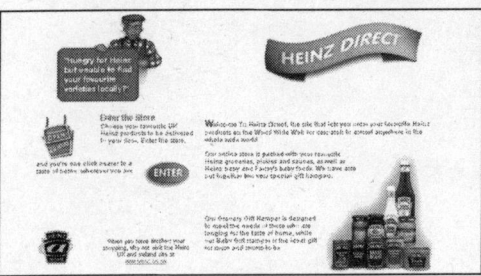

Heinz UK Direct
http://www.heinz-direct.co.uk

Beanz meanz Heinz, and lots of other things on this site that lets you get emergency food hampers if you can't find your favourite Heinz varieties.

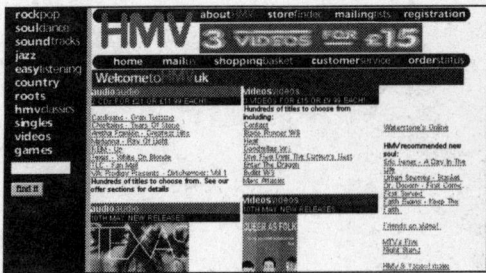

HMV
http://www.hmv.co.uk

A site that's as huge and pink as the high street stores. Not that much in the way of bargains, but worth a browse.

A-Z OF SHOPPING SITES

A-Z OF SHOPPING SITES

I

IBM

http://www.uk.ibm.com

Get all the information about the range of IBM products, and then flex those credit cards and buy one.

Ice Cool

http://www.icecool.co.uk

Supposedly a girl's best friend, diamonds are a nugget of pure, expensive sparkle, but you can pick up some bargains at this site.

A-Z OF SHOPPING SITES

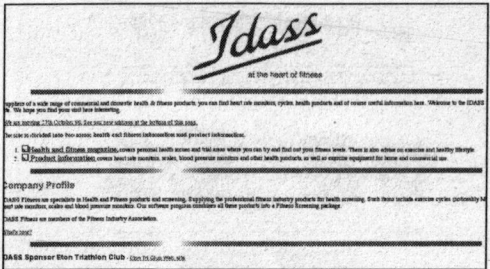

Idass

http://www.idass.com/

Probably only of use to the real fitness freak, the Idass company supply equipment to the professional fitness industry, so at least you know you are getting the best.

iMVS

http://www.imvs.com

Another movie and video shop, but this one also offers other goods such as calendars and computer games.

A-Z OF SHOPPING SITES

Innovations
http://innovations.co.uk

Pretend that you're James Bond, and buy some of these gadgets to make your life easier albeit more cluttered.

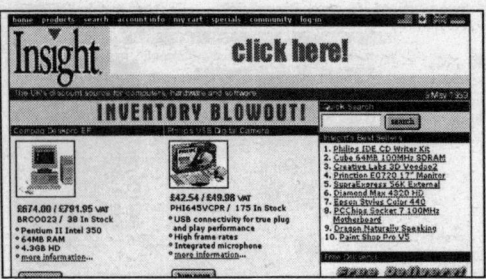

Insight UK
http://www.insight.com

If you want some computers, hardware or software, come to this site for some great discounts.

A-Z OF SHOPPING SITES

International Male
http://www.internationalmale.com

Although the site sounds like the latest boy band, it's actually a site selling all manner of clothes for the male species.

Interflora
http://www.interflora.co.uk

One of the most famous flower services has a very good Web site that makes choosing flowers very easy.

A-Z OF SHOPPING SITES

The Internet Bookshop
http://www.bookshop.co.uk

The site promises savings of up to forty per cent on over 1.4 million book titles from the UK and US.

The Internet Music Shop
http://www.musicsales.co.uk

For all those musicians out there, the Internet Music Shop offers sheet music for you to play your tunes.

A-Z OF SHOPPING SITES

Internet Shopping
http://www.internetshopping.com

An online catalogue of all sorts of goodies, which you can order safe in the knowledge that you will receive a safe service.

The Internet Wallpaper Store
http://www.wallpaperstore.com

Fancy a change from your old magnolia wallpaper? Then come to this site and choose from a wide range of wallpapers and borders and fabrics.

A-Z OF SHOPPING SITES

J

A-Z OF SHOPPING SITES

The Jaguar Collection
http://www.collection.co.uk

Even if you can't afford a real Jaguar, console yourself by picking up spme trinkets from this site.

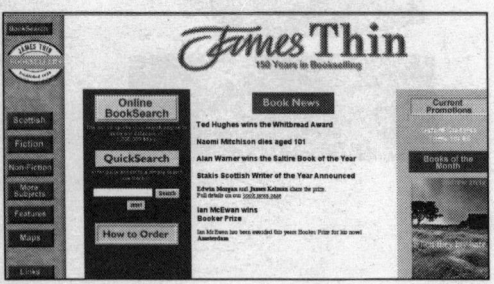

James Thin Booksellers
http://www.jthin.co.uk

For that more refined approach to books, and with a special section on Scottish literature, visit James Thin's site.

A-Z OF SHOPPING SITES

JC Sports
http://www.jcsports.force9.co.uk/

Not to be confused with JD Sports, JC is the supplier of replica shirts, with loads of offers on lots of items.

JCPenney
http://www.jcpenney.com

Experience that American store atmosphere by visiting the JCPenney Web site. You can buy a wide range of goods from here, although it's not as fun as going there in person.

A-Z OF SHOPPING SITES

J

JD Sports
http://www.jdsports.co.uk

Get yourself kitted out in all the latest sporting wears, including the latest in a long line of England strips.

JermynStreet
http://www.jermynstreet.com

A site launched primarily to promote the swanky Jermyn Street in London, you can pick up all manner of luxurious items here.

A-Z OF SHOPPING SITES

Jones Bootmaker
http://www.jonesbootmaker.com

Keep your feet happy, and deck them out in some fantastic footwear from Jones Bootmaker. It's not all boots you know.

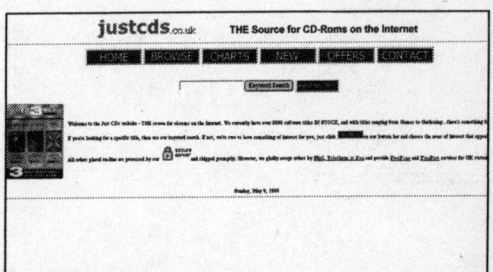

Just CDs
http://www.justcds.co.uk

If it's CD-ROMs you want, this site will suffice. With over 3,000 software titles, you're bound to find something that will appeal.

A-Z OF SHOPPING SITES

K

A-Z OF SHOPPING SITES

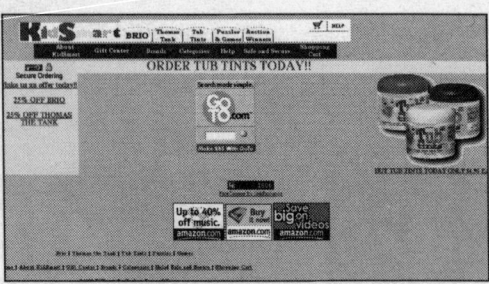

Kids Smart
http://www.kidsmartinc.com

Loads of cool stuff for kids, including paints and toys and *Thomas the Tank Engine*.

Kool Collectables
http://www.koolcollectables.com

After you've seen the TV programme or film, you can read the book, buy the models and wear the t-shirt thanks to this site of kids' TV merchandise.

A-Z OF SHOPPING SITES

K

A-Z OF SHOPPING SITES

A-Z OF SHOPPING SITES

LA Muscle
http://www.lamuscle.com

If you dream of a body like Arnie Shwarzenegger, you will probably find this site useful as it has loads of information for bodybuilders, as well as athletes, and loads of products for you to purchase.

Lantz Stationary
http://www.lantz.ie

Whether it's wedding stationary or Christmas cards, you will find some exquisite designs on this site.

A-Z OF SHOPPING SITES

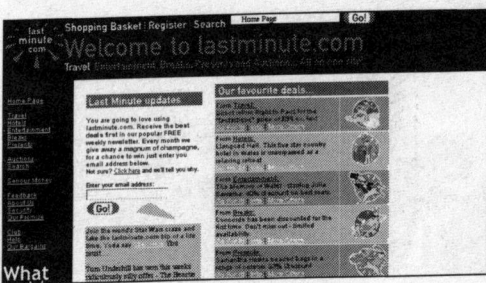

Lastminute.com
http://www.lastminute.com

For those times when you are at the end of your tether, Lastminute.com is there with all the last minute travel deals, so you can pack your bags and leave it all behind.

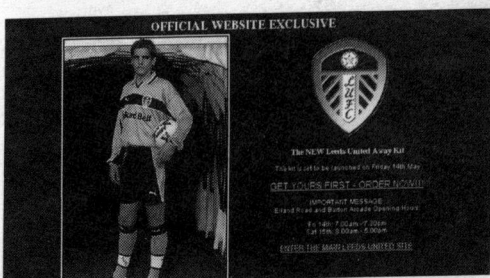

Leeds United FC
http://www.lufc.co.uk

If you're a fan of Leeds football club, and you need to get kitted out in the latest, erm, kit, then this is the place to come.

A-Z OF SHOPPING SITES

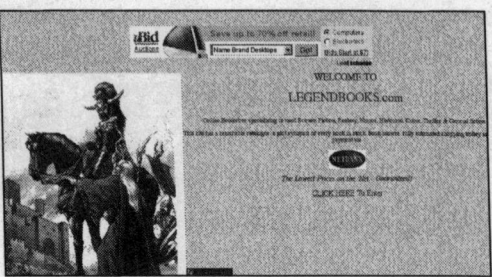

Legendbooks
http://www.legendbooks.com

A site that can easily keep you supplied with science fiction and fantasy literature for the rest of your life.

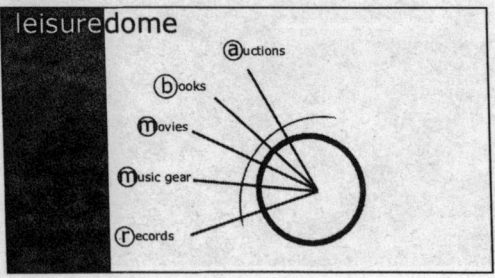

Leisuredome
http://www.leisuredome.com

You can pick up a wide array of goods from Leisuredome, from books, to movies to records – you can even auction.

A-Z OF SHOPPING SITES

Letterbox
http://www.l-box.co.uk
One of the best things in the world is getting a parcel through the post, and that's exactly what you can give with this site specialising in original children's presents.

Littlestar
http://www.littlestar.co.uk
You can sift through over 100,000 different CD titles at this site, and the best thing is, all the prices are free of any VAT.

A-Z OF SHOPPING SITES

Lombard
http://www.lombard.co.uk

Although not really a shopping site as such, Lomvard provides loans for that potential shopping spree.

London Property News
http://www.lpn.co.uk/

If you're thinking of moving to the big smoke, you're going to need some help finding somewhere to live. That's where London Property News comes in, which will have you settled in a new abode in no time.

A-Z OF SHOPPING SITES

L

A-Z OF SHOPPING SITES

A-Z OF SHOPPING SITES

MacDonald's
http://www.smokedproduce.co.uk

Nothing to do with a scary clown with red hair, this site offers some very fine smoked products from Scotland. You can chose from fish, haggis, game, meats and cheese.

MacWarehouse
http://www.macwarehouse.co.uk

Never be at a loss of what Mac product to buy – this site is overflowing with goodies for all you Mac lovers.

A-Z OF SHOPPING SITES

Made In Sheffield
http://www.made-in-sheffield.com

Sheffield stainless steel is among the bets in the world, and you can pick up lovely shiny things from this site.

The Magazine Shop
http://www.magazineshop.co.uk

Subscribe to all your favourite magazines from this site, and have a nose through the sample magazines if you're not sure what you like.

A-Z OF SHOPPING SITES

Magpie Records
http://www.magpierecords.co.uk

A handy site that gives you access to all the releases that are in the charts, or are just sought after.

Maurice Abrahams
http://www.menswear.ie

Sometimes a cheap suit just isn't enough, and for those occasions, there's Maurice Abrahams. This Irish company provides some very fine suits indeed.

A-Z OF SHOPPING SITES

MCM Electronics
http://www.mcmelectronics.com

If you are an electronics enthusiast or professional, MCM Electronics stocks more than 40,000 products to keep you happy.

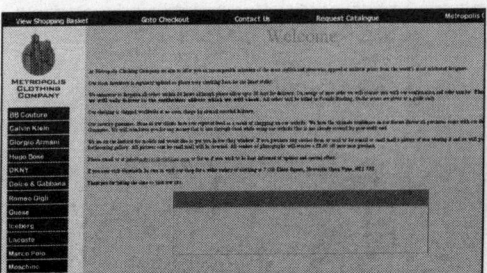

Metropolis Clothing Company
http://www.metropolis-clothing.com

For some great deals on designer fashion, visit the big Metropolis. Most items are shipped within 24 hours, and there's no extra charge for airmail recorded delivery.

A-Z OF SHOPPING SITES

Microsoft Expedia UK

http://expedia.msn.co.uk

You can not only do a thorough search for plane tickets from this site, but you can also buy your tickets online.

MicroWarehouse

http://www.microwarehouse.co.uk

Part of the same ilk as MacWarehouse, MicroWarehouse supplies no end of PC goodies, and even sells office furniture.

A-Z OF SHOPPING SITES

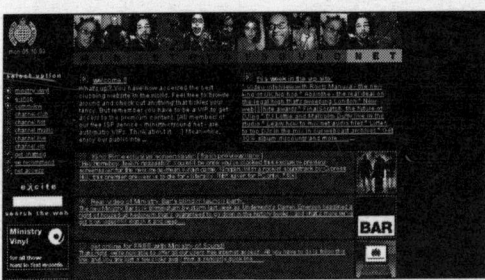

Ministry of Sound
http://www.ministryofsound.co.uk

Get all clubbed up, and visit the Ministry's online shop for loads and loads of goodies that will make you shake your booty.

Molloy's Liquor Stores
http://www.liquorstore.ie

An Irish off-licence chain, Molloy's offers a wide range of beers, wines and spirits to get you charged up.

A-Z OF SHOPPING SITES

Morgan Computer Co
http://www.morgancomputers.co.uk

You can pick up some great bargains at this site, which specialises in end of line computers and peripherals.

MotherNature.com
http://www.mothernature.com

For those who like their beauty products to be 100 per cent natural, MotherNature is there to help. From moisturiser to shampoo, there's plenty to pamper.

A-Z OF SHOPPING SITES

The Movie Zone
http://www.moviezone.co.uk

Fed up with trundling down to your local Blockbusters? Head for Movie Zone, where you can not only buy all your favourite films, but you can rent them, too.

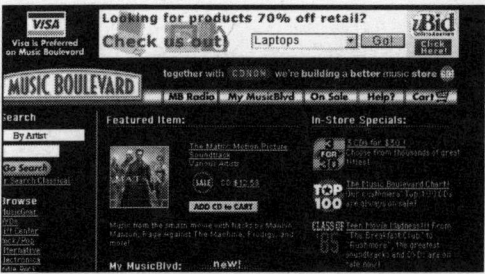

Music Boulevard
http://www.musicblvd.com

Now part of the CDnow group, Music Boulevard may not be as extensive as its partner, but there are still some decent bargains to be found.

A-Z OF SHOPPING SITES

A-Z OF SHOPPING SITES

Nancy Carlson

http://www.nancycarlson.com

Illustrator Nancy Carlson has her own Web site for kids interested in drawing, and also sells the supplies to go with it.

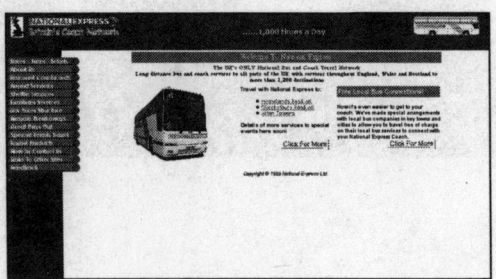

National Express

http://www.eurolines.co.uk

Get yourself out and about by hopping on a coach and visiting somewhere exciting. Coaches offer excellent value for money, and you can book your trip here.

A-Z OF SHOPPING SITES

National History Bookshop
http://www.nhbs.co.uk

With loads of books that cover every facet of th enatural world, you'll soon have more knowledge than David Attenborough.

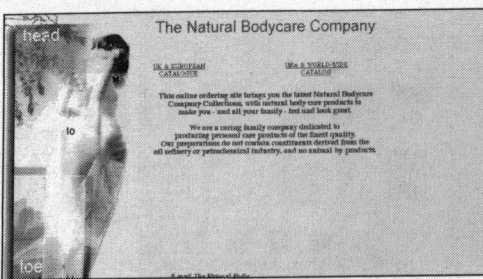

Natural Bodycare Company
http://www.natural-bodycare.com

Completely natural cosmetics that have also been produced without any testing on animals. There is a good range of products, and all orders are secure.

A-Z OF SHOPPING SITES

Naxos Audio Books
http://www.naxos.co.uk/audiobooks

This site supplies all manner of audio books, from fiction to poetry to drama. Pick up the latest talking tomes here.

Net Megastore
http://www.net-megastore.co.uk

Loads of stuff can be found on this site, from console games to books to MiniDiscs. If you live in the UK or Channel Islands, you can benefit from free postage and packaging, too

A-Z OF SHOPPING SITES

Nethergate Wines
http://www.wine-merchant.com

If you want some tasty tipple, Nethergate Wines can supply you with all you need. You can buy mixed wine cases, and even borrow glasses, so it's all here.

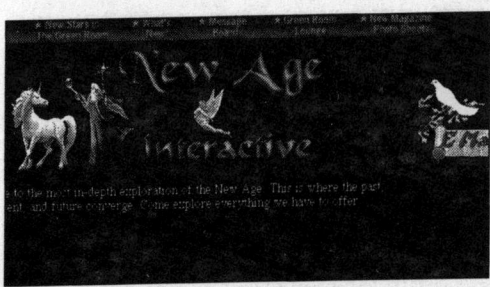

New Age Interactive
http://www.newageinteractive.com

Not only can you get your palm read, take part in online tarot, or check up on the world's superstitions, you can also buy some excellent New Age goods.

A-Z OF SHOPPING SITES

Newcastle United
http://ssl.nufc.co.uk/nufc

If you're a fan of Newcastle, get yourself to this site and deck yourself out in black and white stripes.

New World Creations
http://www.nwcreations.com

You can buy either commissioned artwork, or prints from this site that deals with images of a more spiritual nature.

A-Z OF SHOPPING SITES

Nintendo Direct
http://www.nintendodirect.com

If your nights are bathed in the glow of an N64, you'll find that this is an excellent site for picking up some quality bargains to keep you amused.

Nostalgia Store
http://www.nostalgia.co.uk

For those whisty days of yesteryear, the Nostalgia Store is here with loads of products that will bring memories flooding back.

A-Z OF SHOPPING SITES

Nottingham Lace
http://www.nottingham-lace.co.u

If you know of a lady that would love some lace (and we don't mean dodgy underwear) you can buy all sorts of goodies from this site.

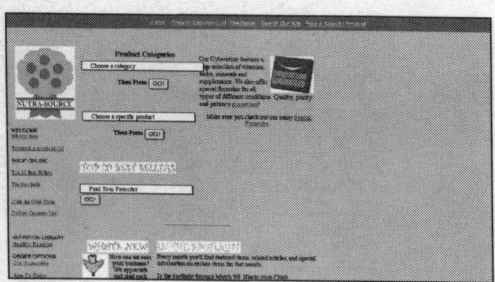

Nutrasource
http://www.nutrasource.com

This site features a wide range of vitamins, herbs, minerals and supplements.

A-Z OF SHOPPING SITES

NYSNY

http://www.nystyle.com

A site full of tricky clothes, that magically change from day to evening separates with just a swish of some fabric.

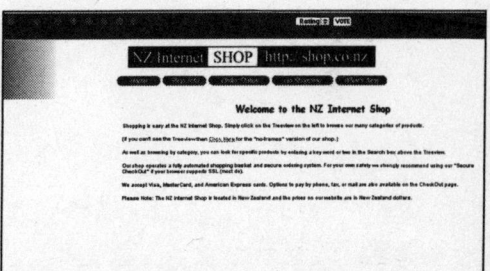

NZ Internet Bookshop

http://www.shop.co.nz/shop/shop.cgi

If it's children's or computer books that you're after, this site will supply you with all that you need.

A-Z OF SHOPPING SITES

A-Z OF SHOPPING SITES

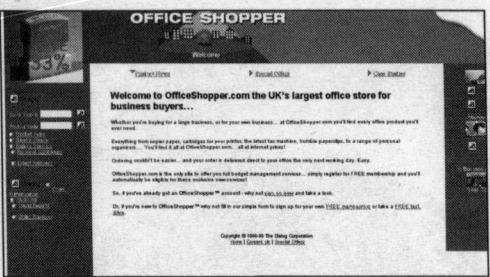

OfficeShopper
http://www.officeshopper.com

OfficeShopper calls itself the UK's largest office store, and there is certainly lots on offer, with some items on discount.

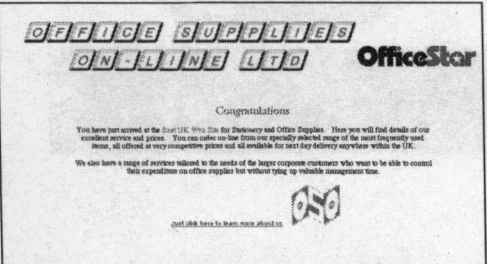

Office Supplies On-Line
http://www.office-supplies.co.uk

With the most frequently used items on offer, and a next day delivery service on most items, Office Supplies On-Line is an excellent site.

A-Z OF SHOPPING SITES

Offtek

http://www.offtek.co.uk

Suppliers of memory for all sorts of machines, including desktops, notebooks and printers, all delivered free of charge.

Old Glory

http://www.oldglory.com

A really good site with loads of merchandise for classic rock bands, as well as TV shows and popular culture.

A-Z OF SHOPPING SITES

O

OldTimer

http://www.oldtimer.ndirect.co.uk

OldTimer is a company specialising in quality classic and sports cars. You can also buy miscellaneous items to complete the feeling.

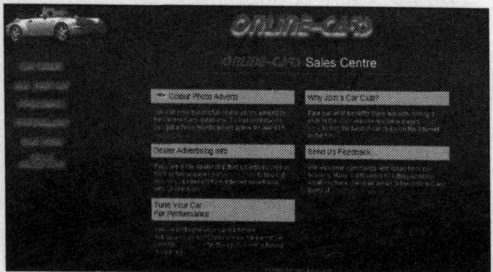

Online-Cars

http://www.online-cars.com

Just point and click, and within no time, this site will display any used cars that fit in with what you want.

A-Z OF SHOPPING SITES

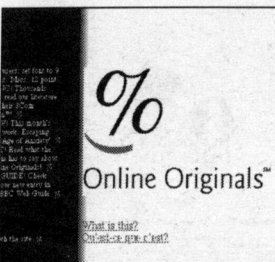

Online Originals
http://www.onlineoriginals.com

A publishing company that operates solely on the Internet. Simply browse through the list of works, make your purchase and you will receive the text by digital format.

Open Group
http://www.opengroup.com

A site with currently more than 600,000 titles on its database, you can buy anything from computer titles to cookery books.

A-Z OF SHOPPING SITES

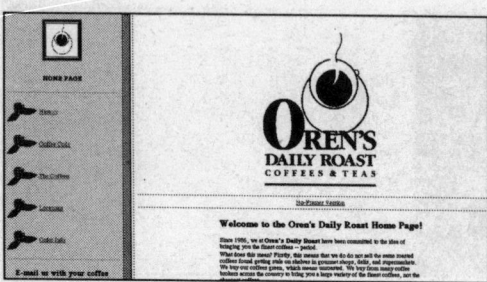

Oren's Daily Roast
http://www.orensdailyroast.com

If you like your coffee to be of the finest quality, then get your caffeine-ridden body to this site for beans galore.

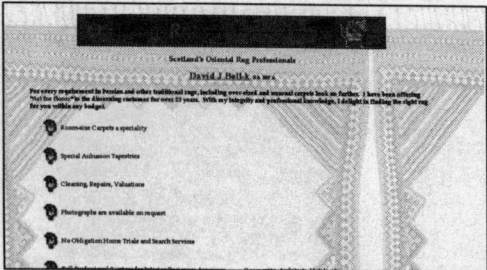

Oriental Rugs of Distinction
http://www.orientalcarpets.co.uk

A great site for rugs of all shapes and sizes – from traditional Persian to other traditional rugs – you're floor never looked so good.

A-Z OF SHOPPING SITES

Original Image Company
http://www.oicuk.com

Decorate your house with images of London, from this company offering black and white photos of the big smoke.

Oxford University Press
http://www.oup.co.uk

You won't find any Mills and Boon-type titles from this company, but you will get some excellent deals

A-Z OF SHOPPING SITES

A-Z OF SHOPPING SITES

P

A-Z OF SHOPPING SITES

Past Perfect
http://www.pastperfect.com

If you're a fan of the music that came out of the 20s, 30s and 40s, you'll love this site.

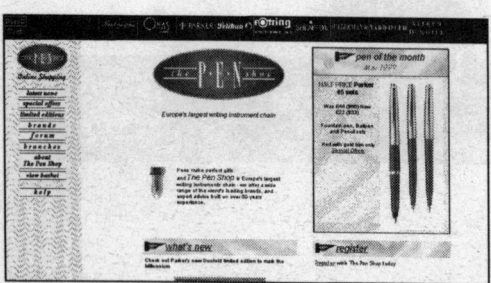

The Pen Shop
http://www.penshop.co.uk

Whether you have a penchant for Parker, or a soft spot for Sheaffer, there's plenty of pens on this site to keep you happy.

A-Z OF SHOPPING SITES

Penguin
http://www.penguin.co.uk
One of the most famous publishers in the world has an excellent online ordering service, so you can read away the days.

Pentagram
http://www.psinet.co.uk/pentagram
Pentagram will sort out all your Pagan and Occult needs, with its thorough online store that stocks all sorts of goodies.

A-Z OF SHOPPING SITES

The Pet's Pyjamas
http://www.pets-pyjamas.co.uk

Complete with an endorsement from Wendy Turner, this is a great site to buy your pets some presents.

The Place to Bee
http://www.beeplace.com

For all things straight from the hive, The Place to Bee sells everything from candles to skincare to books. You'll be as busy as a bee in no time.

A-Z OF SHOPPING SITES

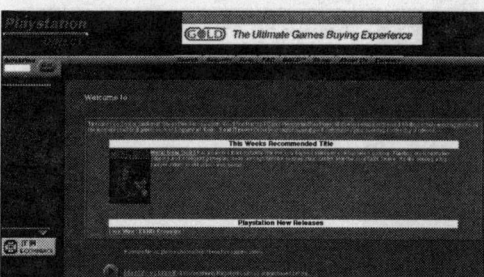

Playstation Direct
http://www.PlaystationDirect.co.uk/

An excellent site where you can not only buy all the latest Playstation games, but you can join a mailing list to get all the cheats!

Porcupine Books
http://www.porcupine.demon.co.uk

The Web site of an Essex business specialising in second-hand science fiction, fantasy and horror books.

A-Z OF SHOPPING SITES

Principles
http://www.principles.co.uk

The famous high street store has an excellent Web site where you can buy some excellent clobber.

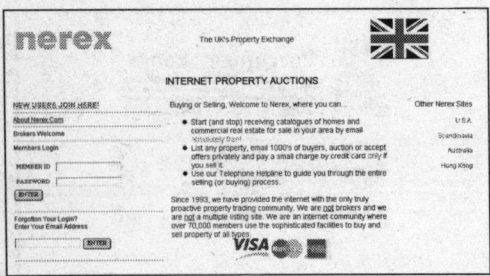

Property Find
http://www.propertyfind.co.uk

Claiming to be the only online property auction in the UK, Property Find sells both residential and commercial properties.

A-Z OF SHOPPING SITES

Psion
http://www.21store.com/psion

Mnufacturers of some extremely handy little gadgets, Psion has a very simple site for you to buy all your modern models.

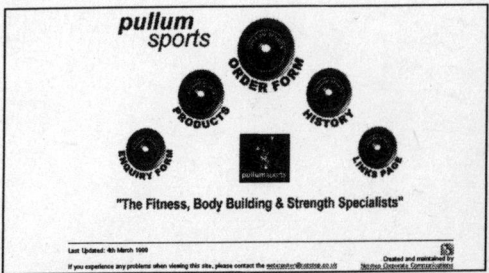

Pullum Sports
http://www.powerlifting.com/pullum

This company supplies weightlifting equipment to a lot of the fitness industry, and now offers you the chance to get some barbells to be reckoned with.

A-Z OF SHOPPING SITES

A-Z OF SHOPPING SITES

QAC Glass Engraving
http://www.

Located in Sutton Coldfield, the Queen Alexandra College offers a glass engraving service, so you can have portraits blasted onto glass products.

qxl
http://www.qxl.com

An online auction site for Europe, you simply log on, make you bid and if you're successful, you just have to wait for your goods to arrive.

A-Z OF SHOPPING SITES

QVCUK.com
http://www.qvcuk.com

A site from the marvellously cheesy QVC home shopping channel, with lots of glitzy wares to buy.

A-Z OF SHOPPING SITES

R

A-Z OF SHOPPING SITES

Racing Green
http://www.racinggreen.co.uk

Bringing the London store online, you can pick up some quality clothing at his site, and the summer 1999 range is online, too.

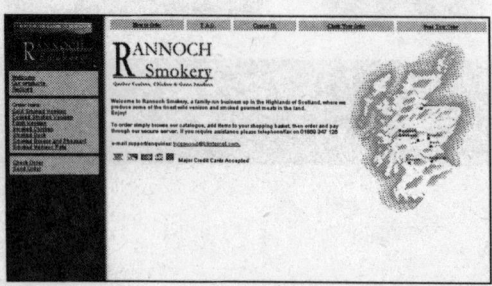

Rannoch Smokery
http://www.rannochsmokery.co.uk

Lots of smoked food on offer, including venison, chicken and game. More posh than your average haddock.

A-Z OF SHOPPING SITES

Reckless Woman
http://www.recklesswoman.com

Billed as a site for women who like to have fun, when we visited, the special of the day was a red rubber latex mini skirt. Nice.

Recollections
http://www.recollections.co.uk

Take a trip down memory lane with this site that offers loads of music by some classic bands, including Abba, Black Sabbath and Rolling Stones.

A-Z OF SHOPPING SITES

R

Reflections
http://www.globalnet.co.uk/~pblake/holshop.html

An unusual site that sells holograms. So if the thought of a face following you around the room appeals, you know where to come.

Mackintosh Collection (Explorer)

Rennie Mackintosh
http://www.studio-jupiter.com

If you're a fan of the distinctive style of Rennie Mackintosh, this site will delight you with all it has on offer, which includes jewellery, hardwood and mirrors.

A-Z OF SHOPPING SITES

Ridleys
http://www.ridleys.co.uk

Order all your favourite ales from this Essex brewer, and relax, safe in the knowledge that your beer is winging its way to you

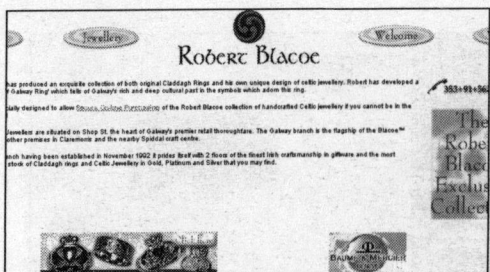

Robert Blacoe
http://www.blacoe.com

You can buy original Claddagh rings from this site, as well as celtic jewellery designed by Robert Blacoe

A-Z OF SHOPPING SITES

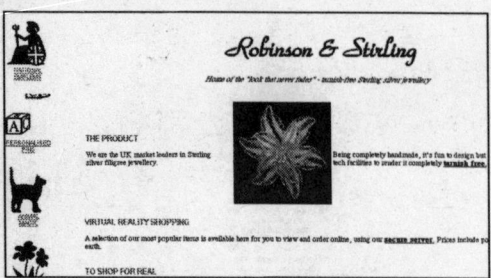

Robinson and Stirling
http://www.robinson-and-stirling.com

Makers of filigree sterling silver jewellery, Robinson and Stirling offers some unusual designs and the prices include postage to anywhere in the world.

Rugs Direct
http://ds.dial.pipex.com/town/parade/nr78

There's loads of rugs on offer at this site, and when we visited, there were offers on Chinese Dynasty and Indian Beytana.

A-Z OF SHOPPING SITES

R

A-Z OF SHOPPING SITES

A-Z OF SHOPPING SITES

Sainsbury's
http://www.sainsburys.co.uk

Although it's only available to certain areas, online grocery shopping is gradually growing, and you can get a taste of what's involved here.

Sax Design
http://www.saxdesign.com

People often forget about ties, but Sax Design sells nothing but ties. If you buy two ties, you get a five per cent discount, which increases to 10 per cent if you buy three or more.

A-Z OF SHOPPING SITES

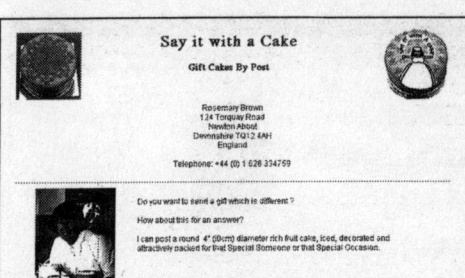

Say it with a Cake
http://www.devon.directory.co.uk

Sometimes nothing can beat a cake, especially if you get sent one in the post. Which is exactly what you get with this service – gift cakes by post.

Sci-Fi UK
http://www.scifi-uk.com

As th name suggests, you can find all manner of science fiction products on this site, separated according to show.

A-Z OF SHOPPING SITES

Scot Books

http://www.scotbooks.com

If you're a fan of Scottish literature, check out this site which consists entirely of books from Scottish publishers.

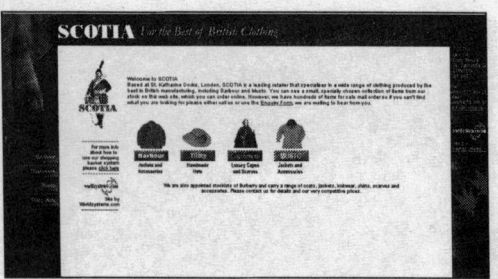

Scotia

http://www.scotia.uk.com

From the design consisting of tartan, tweed and leaves, there can be little doubt that this company specialises in outdoor fashion, and all the best names are included.

A-Z OF SHOPPING SITES

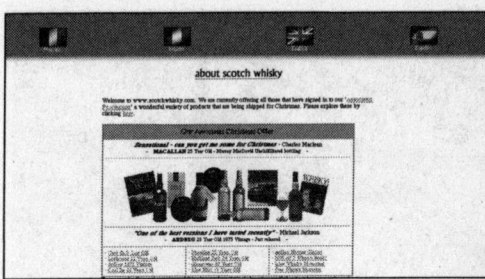

Scotch Whiskey
http://www.scotchwhisky.com

Not only do you get lots of information about whiskey, but you get the chance to order some of the golden stuff, too.

Screen Edge
http://www.screenedge.com

An excellent site that sells videos from film makers that definitely wouldn't be welcome in Hollywood. Titles include *Cannibal: The Musical*, *Criminal* and *Addicted to Murder*.

A-Z OF SHOPPING SITES

Sharper Image
http://www.sharperimage.com

Bit of a mish-mash of products, with cameras, clothing, model cars and toys all on offer. You also get $2 off your first order.

Shipton&Heneage
http://www.shiphen.com

If it's quality shoes that you're after, the hand-made attire for your feet provided by Shipton and Heneage should suffice.

A-Z OF SHOPPING SITES

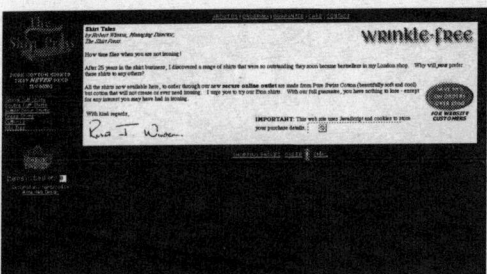

The Shirt Press
http://www.shirt-press.demon.co.uk

Ironing is loved by no one, but thanks to non-iron clothes, you no longer have to spend hours hunched over a board. This site supplies you with all the shirts you could want.

Shopping.com
http://shopping.com

There's loads of products on offer from this online catalogue. You want consumer electronics, or an alien in galaxy motion lamp, you've got it.

A-Z OF SHOPPING SITES

Shopping Centre.net
http://www.shoppingcentre.net/

A collection of lots of different stand-alone shopping sites, Shopping Centre.net saves you having to trawl through the Net.

ShoppersUniverse
http://www.shoppersuniverse.com

Part of Great Universal, and split into 20 different areas covering 40,000 different products, the site is so huge it makes you dizzy.

A-Z OF SHOPPING SITES

Sports Connection
http://www.sportsconnection.co.uk

A well designed site that has all the essential sports wear equipment that you will need, including footwear, accessories, even replica shirts.

Sportspages
http://www.sportspages.co.uk

If it's sports goods you're after, Sportspages is just the site for you. With books and videos, your eyes will be thoroughly worked out.

A-Z OF SHOPPING SITES

A-Z OF SHOPPING SITES

Tack and Ski
http://www.tackandski.co.uk

If you like horse riding, skiing or other outdoor activities, this site sells all the clothing, equipment and accessories that you will need at competitive prices.

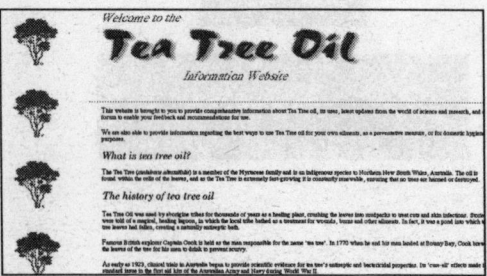

Tea Tree Oil
http://www.teatree.co.uk

An information Web site dedicated to this wonderful oil which can heal just about any skin abrasion there is. Buy your stash online.

A-Z OF SHOPPING SITES

The Teddington Cheese Online
http://www.teddingtoncheese.co.uk

With over 130 varieties of cheese, the Teddington Cheese Company is an excellent place to come if you want something more exciting than mild chedder.

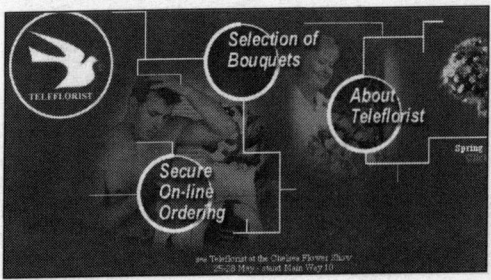

Teleflorist
http://www.teleflorist.co.uk

With its beautiful selection of bouquets, Teleflorist is the ideal place to come if you want to surprise someone you love.

A-Z OF SHOPPING SITES

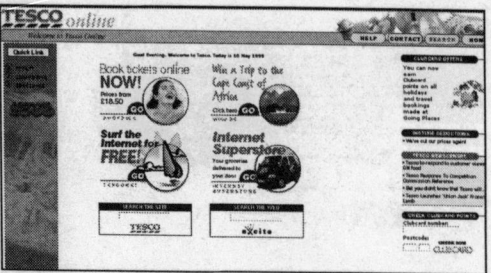

Tesco
http://www.tesco.co.uk

As with Sainsbury's, the online shopping service from Tesco is only available in a limited area, but if you live within those areas, you should definitely take advantage of it.

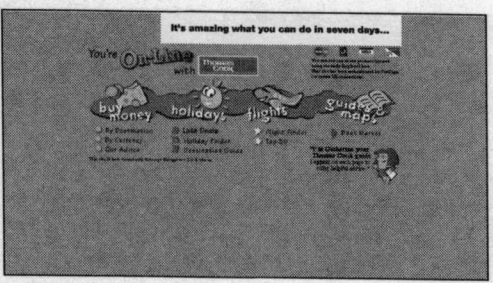

Thomas Cook
http://www.thomascook.co.uk

Organise your holiday online with Thomas Cook, and take advantage of some late deals.

A-Z OF SHOPPING SITES

Thorntons
http://www.thorntons.co.uk

Making its chocolate heaven since 1911, Thorntons has a lovely site where you can order scrummy chocolates.

Ticketmaster
http://www.ticketmaster.co.uk

Buy all you concert, theatre and show tickets online through one of the most infamous ticket suppliers.

A-Z OF SHOPPING SITES

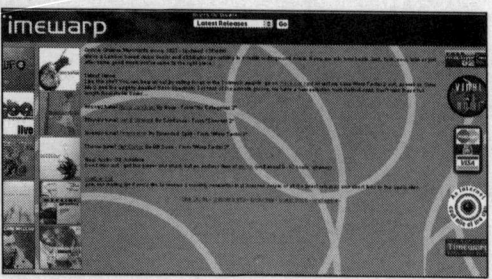

Timewarp Records
http://www.tunes.co.uk/timewarp

Get jazzed up this summer with Timewarp records and the groovy tunes supplied on the site.

Titanic Leisure
http://www.titanic-leisure.com

A small range of clothes that celebrate the atmosphere of the White Star Liner, presumably before it sank.

A-Z OF SHOPPING SITES

Tots 2 Teens
http://www.shoppersuniverse.com/su/main.asp?cat=677&prod_id=&link_id=150&zone_id=&mscs_sid=R1JFG48X0WSH2JB400C7J2SWJJ1RMUHX

This site has clothes for boys and girls, and also sells pushchairs, sports gear and shoes.

Tower Records
http://www.towereurope.com

If you prefer to buy your music from Tower Records, you can now do it online.

A-Z OF SHOPPING SITES

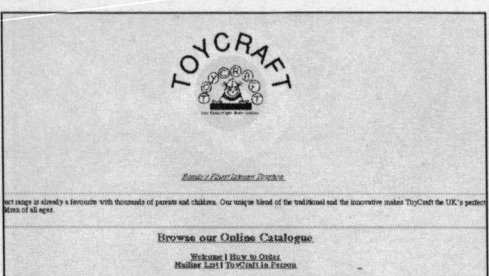

ToyCraft
http://catalog.com/uk/toy

You'll find good quality toys on this site, which seems to care about building children's imaginations rather than bowing to the latest fad.

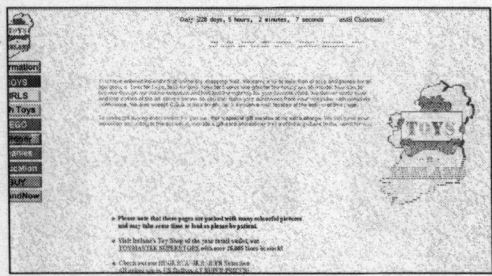

Toy-n-Ireland
http://www.ireland-now.com

Ireland's first online store, including some rather foxy Irish toys, such as musical Leprechaun.

A-Z OF SHOPPING SITES

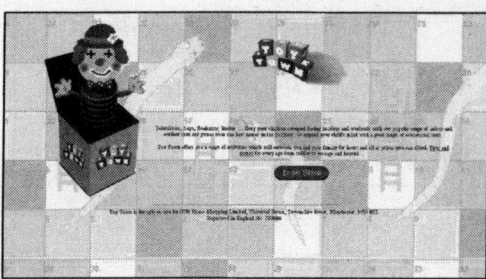

ToyTown
http://www.toytown.co.uk

A huge range of indoor and outdoor games that will keep the little ones amused and out from under your feet.

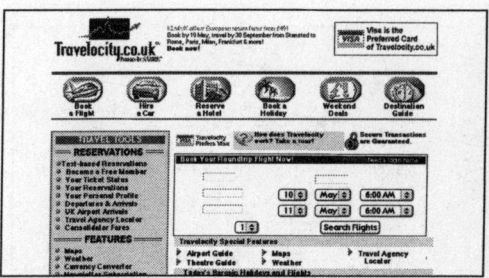

Travelocity
http://www.travelocity.co.uk

You can do everything from this site, including book a flight, hire a car and reserve a hotel.

A-Z OF SHOPPING SITES

TUCOWS
http://www.tucows.com

Claiming to have the biggest selection of Internet software, TUCOWS is a great place to stock up on the latest Mac, Windows and OS/2 software.

Tyler's Garden Centre
http://www.tylers.co.uk/

You can buy everything to make a resplendent garden, from furniture, to tools and fencing, and of course, those all-important plants.

A-Z OF SHOPPING SITES

T

A-Z OF SHOPPING SITES

A-Z OF SHOPPING SITES

UK Property
http://www.uk-property.com

From this site, you can browse properties throughout the UK, and even dip your toe in fields that are further away.

UK Shopping City
http://www.ukshops.co.uk/

There's a vast range of shops on this site, ranging from retail through to fun and games and technology. You can also search European sites.

A-Z OF SHOPPING SITES

Unbeatable
http://www.unbeatable.co.uk

Loads of camera bargains for those budding David Baileys out there.

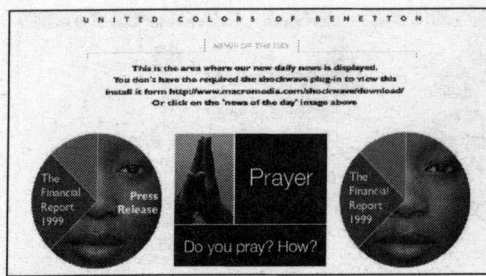

United Colours of Benetton
http://www.benetton.com/

This is the official site of the Italian clothes designers, so if you're a fan of the clothes, check it out.

A-Z OF SHOPPING SITES

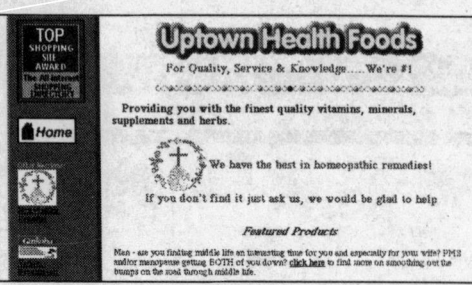

Uptown Health
http://www.getset.com/uptown/uptown.html

A very thorough site that deals in vitamins, minerals supplements and herbs. All good stuff.

Uptown Records
http://www.uptownrecords.com/

Established for over four years, Uptown Records is one of the leading dance record stores and you can buy all the tunes online.

A-Z OF SHOPPING SITES

U

A-Z OF SHOPPING SITES

A-Z OF SHOPPING SITES

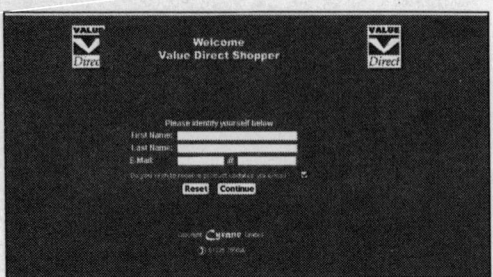

Value Direct
http://www.value-direct.co.uk

After a short registration process, you can search for kitchen appliances on the site, and receive information about new products by email.

Vegetarian Recipes
http://www.veg.org

Lots of vegetarian goodies to buy, all of them marvellous.

A-Z OF SHOPPING SITES

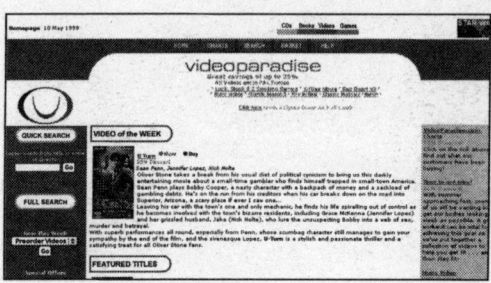

Videoparadise
http://www.videoparadise.com

Lots and lots of videos to chose from, many with some decent discounts. When we visited, there was a 25 per cent discount on Oliver Stone's U Turn

Vodafone
http://www.vodafone-retail.co.uk

If you're thinking about buying a new phone, Vodafone are one of the most recognisable names, and you can buy directly from the site.

A-Z OF SHOPPING SITES

A-Z OF SHOPPING SITES

Wadsworth
http://www2.wadsworth.co.uk

If you want some computer networking, voive, audio and broadcast products, this is the site to visit.

Warr's
http://www.harley-davidson-london.co.uk

This company sells and service Harley Davidsons, and although you can't buy a bike online, you can always buy a t-shirt.

A-Z OF SHOPPING SITES

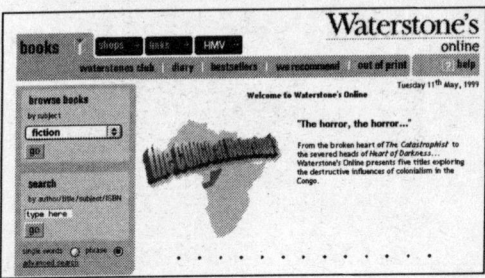

Waterstone's
http://www.waterstones.co.uk
One of the best bookshops in the high street also has a very good Web site where you can buy all the bestsellers, and make use of the second hand book service.

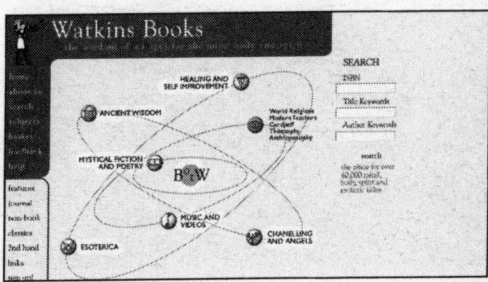

Watkins
http://www.watkinsbooks.com
A bookshop specialising in literature for the mind, body and spirit, you will find no end of inspiration here.

A-Z OF SHOPPING SITES

A-Z OF SHOPPING SITES

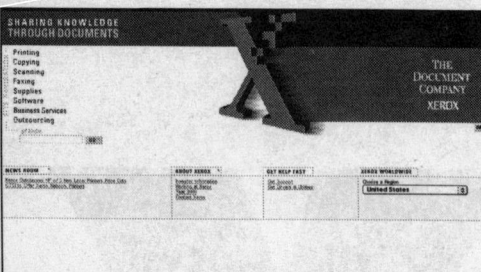

Xerox

http://www.xerox.com

You can buy all manner of electrical goods from this site, and get loads of information, too.

xplore

http://www.xplore.com/xplore500/medium/shopping.html

Basically a search engine, it also provides a useful list of secure online shops.

A-Z OF SHOPPING SITES

X

A-Z OF SHOPPING SITES

A-Z OF SHOPPING SITES

Yahoo! Shopping
http://shopping.uk.yahoo.com

A good place to start if you're new to online shopping, as it provides plenty of links to secure sites.

YiXing
http://www.yixing.com

For that unusual gift, why not visit YiXing.com and buy one of the lovely zisha teapots from China? There are some beautiful designs and you can also buy loose leaf tea from the site.

A-Z OF SHOPPING SITES

Youngs Menswear
http://www.seven.net/youngs

An independent retailer of menswear located in Gloucester, you can also browse and order from the range of goods online.

Y'rus
http://www.yrus.com

A rather flash range of bikini designs, which will get your holiday off to a scorching start.

A-Z OF SHOPPING SITES

A-Z OF SHOPPING SITES

Zardoz

http://www.zardozbooks.co.uk

If you have an interest in out-of-print or collectible books, Zardoz claims to be Europe's largest specialist dealer, and it also has a variety of picture cards.

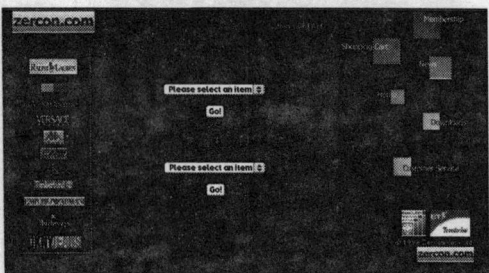

Zercon.com

https://www.zercon.com

Selling swanky designer gear, you can pick up your Versace clobber and become one of the beautiful people.

A-Z OF SHOPPING SITES

Zoria Farms
http://www.zoria.com

For that 'spent too long in the bath' wrinkly experience, visit this site and buy some of the dried fruits on offer. There's also chocolates, nuts and gift baskets for sale.

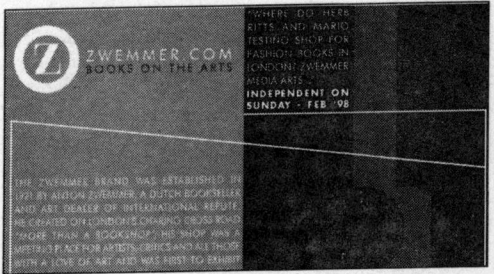

Zwemmer
http://www.zwemmer.co.uk

This site deals with books on the arts, so if you fancy yourself as part of the Bloomsbury brigade, yu know where to come for the information.

APPENDIX

Whether you want to do a general search for shopping sites, or have a specific store in mind, here's a list of useful resources

A-Z OF SHOPPING SITES

Finding shopping sites

Hopefully, this book will keep the most ardent Net shopper busy for a while, but if we haven't covered products you're interested in, try doing a Web search with these search directories and engines. Some have dedicated shopping sections, available from the welcome screen.

Yahoo! (http://www.yahoo.co.uk)
UKplus (http://www.ukplus.com)
AltaVista (http://www.altavista.digital.com)
Excite (http://www.excite.com)
HotBot (http://www.hotbot.com)
Infoseek (http://www.infoseek.com)
Lycos (http://www.lycos.co.uk)
Ask Jeeves (http://www.askjeeves.com)
MetaCrawler (http://www.metacrawler.com)

Web shopping channels

Increasingly, service providers are including shopping 'channels' with plenty of goods for sale.

AOL (http://www.aol.co.uk)
CompuServe (http://www.compuserve.co.uk)
LineOne (http://www.lineone.net)
MSN (http://www.msn.com)
UK Online (http://www.ukonline.co.uk)
Virgin Net (http://www.virgin.net/shopping)

A-Z OF SHOPPING SITES

Web shopping malls

Buyer's Index (http://www.buyersindex.com)
Search 9,600 Web shopping sites and US mail-order catalogues.

Shop Guide (http://www.shopguide.co.uk)
Includes over 90 secure online shops, all based in the UK.

Shopper's Universe (http://www.shoppersuniverse.co.uk)
This site lets you search from thousands of brand-name products.

Shops on the Net (http://www.shopsonthenet.com)
Search by shop name, URL, subject or location.

BarclaySquare (http://www.barclaysquare.co.ukj)
A long-established site that places particular emphasis on security.

Legal issues/consumer rights

The Law Society (http://www.lawsoc.org.uk/home.html)
Office of Fair Trading (http://www.oft.gov.uk/)

Secure online transactions

Mastercard (http://www.mastercard.com)
Visa (http://www.visa.com)
SET (http://www.setco.org)
Verisign (http://www.verisign.org)